Keep Coming,
Holy Spirit

To churches large and small

all over the world

who have been called

to treasure the blessing of revival

and whose only prayer is now

"Keep coming, Holy Spirit!"

OTHER BOOKS BY MELINDA FISH

Adult Children and the Almighty
I Can't Be an Addict—I'm a Christian
I'm So Tired of Acting Spiritual
Restoring the Wounded Woman
The River Is Here

Keep Coming, Holy Spirit

Living in the Heart of Revival

Melinda Fish

Chosen Books

A Division of Baker Book House Co
Grand Rapids, Michigan 49516

© 2001 by Melinda Fish

Published by Chosen Books
a division of Baker Book House Company
P.O. Box 6287, Grand Rapids, MI 49516-6287

Printed in the United States of America

Library of Congress Cataloging-in-Publication Data

Fish, Melinda.
    Keep coming, Holy Spirit : living in the heart of revival / Melinda Fish.
            p.   cm.
    Includes bibliographical references.
    ISBN 0-8007-9282-3 (pbk.)
    1. Revivals. I. Title.
BV3790 .F542   2002
269′.24—dc21   2001047210

Unless otherwise noted, Scripture is taken from the NEW AMERICAN STANDARD BIBLE ®. Copyright © The Lockman Foundation 1960, 1962, 1963, 1968, 1971, 1972, 1973, 1975, 1977, 1995. Used by permission.

Scripture marked niv is taken from the HOLY BIBLE, NEW INTERNATIONAL VERSION®. NIV®. Copyright © 1973, 1978, 1984 by International Bible Society. Used by permission of Zondervan Publishing House. All rights reserved.

Scripture marked tev is taken from the Good News Bible, Today's English Version. Copyright © American Bible Society 1966, 1971, 1976, 1992. Used by permission.

Scripture marked kjv is taken from the King James Version of the Bible.

For current information about all releases from Baker Book House, visit our web site:

http://www.bakerbooks.com

Contents

Foreword

What is it that we really value about our relationship with God? Having our sins forgiven? Receiving the gift of eternal life? Knowing the peace that comes to the soul by receiving the Prince of Peace? Studying and knowing the Word of God? Having a successful ministry?

While these things are important, even essential, there is something missing and often overlooked by many in the Body of Christ: having an intimate relationship with God that flows from experiencing the presence of the Lord deep in your heart and soul. This is, after all, where Jesus is taking us—to the Father: "No one comes to the Father except through me" (John 14:6). You and I are invited by the Holy Spirit to enter into a deep and meaningful heart-and-soul-relationship with God, who is Love. This is what the Toronto revival is primarily all about—inviting weary Christians into the refreshing, revitalizing river of the presence of God.

One would search far and wide to find someone who loves this move of the Holy Spirit more than Melinda Fish. She has truly found something she could die for. What is it that revolutionizes a pastor who is incurably disillusioned with life and ministry? An intimate and powerful relationship with the presence of God! Yet questions are asked every day: *Is "Toronto" still going on? If this is God, then why did our church split over it? Why did everything stop happening in our fellowship?* Melinda answers these probing questions and much more.

This book is a practical how-to manual (hard-hitting at times) explaining how essential it is to treasure the presence of the Holy Spirit and let Him lead. The Pharisees of Jesus' day had front-row seats to all His teaching and miracles, yet were unable to see the very thing they claimed to be praying for: Emmanuel, God with us! The Pharisees of today are still unable to see, yet it is being shouted from the housetops. Melinda tells us through her own wonderful experiences and deep insights how God intends revival to continue on and on and on. It is all backed up with the seasoning that comes from serving God faithfully throughout many dry years—years that brought her to the brink of desperation.

Many will relate only too well as Melinda describes the depth of pain and disillusionment that made her desperate enough to go to Toronto. She pauses with sober reflection, saying, "What if we had missed this? What if we had started but not continued?" This book will help you troubleshoot your own experience with God, or lack thereof. There is a cost to letting Him be in control, but, oh, the joy that follows! You are admonished to value this "river" as precious, to keep it pure and to let nothing stop it. The tension often is centered around issues of religious striving, people-pleasing and handing control over to God. You will encounter more than one sacred cow that expires under Melinda's pen!

The abiding presence of the Holy Spirit really is the treasure that we seek. And we truly have this treasure in earthen vessels. This is the Father's promised blessing (see Acts 1:4). You, too, can be revolutionized for Jesus and launched into successful ministry. Just know that it all hinges on heartfelt and deeply emotional intimacy with God.

If you are hungry or desperate for more of God's presence or are wondering where you made a wrong turn and somehow missed Him, then this book is must-read. Be warned, though: The velvet hammer of the Holy Spirit will relentlessly go after angers, fears and secret sins of every kind. He wants a Bride who has made herself ready and is deeply in love— heart and soul—with Jesus.

Do your pastor a favor and get him a copy, too. It will turn your church around.

John Arnott, Senior Pastor
Toronto Airport Christian Fellowship

One

Keep Coming, Holy Spirit: Treasuring Revival

Some years ago, I was sick of "ordinary." Even though I served as pastor—and pastor's wife—in a charismatic church, I felt as though I was living in a religious nightmare. The powerful presence of God was missing in our church. It was as though we had become so accustomed to living without His power that we had surrendered to the treadmill of "doing church." Only occasionally would we see an invasion of the truly supernatural, such as when someone was saved or healed. To me the supernatural works of God had a random quality about them, both in our church and elsewhere, and even when something happened, it rarely ever produced any true awe of God.

To be honest, at times I felt abandoned by God. I was not co-laboring with Christ; I was laboring under the sense that if my husband and I did not do it, it would not get done. Everything would fold. And yet I could not plan another women's retreat or attend one more conference. My heart was sick from deferred hope, and my husband, Bill, and I wanted out of the ministry.

By the year 1994 I wondered if I could hang on one more day, plodding through the realm of the religious ordinary. God told Ezekiel that it was the priest's duty to "teach the people the difference between the sacred and the ordinary" (Ezekiel 44:23, TEV). I can see now that in preparing us to receive the sacred, God often prefaces our experiences with Him by a whole lot of "ordinary."

THE RELIGIOUS ORDINARY

It seems contradictory but it is quite possible, in the realm of the religious ordinary, for churches to grow to massive size. People can even be saved because the Lord is faithful to the preaching of the Gospel. Christians can be baptized in the Holy Spirit, move in His gifts and embrace biblically sound doctrine. Leaders can hold citywide Christian events, reach large numbers of listeners through Christian radio and TV. All looks fine on the outside, but in moments of solitude you try to shove aside the sense that there really ought to be more to God than this.

Truly honest ministers know this and sometimes talk about it. I remember that during this time Bill and I had several luncheon dates with another local charismatic minister and his wife. We talked about where God was in all that we were doing. I remember thinking how I had left my career as a high-school teacher to enter the ministry because I was certain I would be led by a supernatural God. And yet nearly twenty years had gone by, and I was lost on a cycle of religious boredom. I did not have the sense that God was even in our services most of the time. Actually, He was not there—that is, not at all the way He could have been—and I could not find out where He was.

We were suffering from a barrenness syndrome, an emotional roller-coaster ride of hope, crisis and disappointment while waiting for dreams to be fulfilled. I had been so long on this roller coaster as far as our church was concerned that it was becoming a lifestyle. We were weary of attending conferences where people discussed church growth, cell groups and even evangelism because there was no way to implement most of what we heard, no way to get "from here to there." And what we were able to implement did not usually last. Our church attendance stood between forty and sixty on Sundays; we took comfort in the fact that more than 80 percent of the churches in America were the same size as ours.

We were not living in known sin. We were faithful to our tasks. We even prophesied about things to come and ministered to the needy. We tithed, gave offerings and sowed liberally into other ministries, but if you had asked me then, I would have had to say that we received very little return on our investment in our church. I knew that cynicism was hardening my heart from all I had been through, and it was quickly turning into despair.

In the spring of 1994, I had major surgery and began to experience panic attacks. I would wake up in the middle of the night trembling in horror of impending doom. I could not shake these attacks no matter how I tried. A desire to see God do the extraordinary was turning into a need for it.

Setting the Stage

During these eighteen years of ministry in Pittsburgh, Bill and I had received numerous prophetic words about a future move of God in our midst. It was often spoken of as "a River" and "the Blessing."

The first of these words came to Bill while we were still in Texas, some weeks before we arrived in Pittsburgh. As he describes it:

> The Lord gave me a vision of waters coming from a mountaintop into the desert and through the doors of a weather-beaten church. The water brought life wherever it went with trees and flowers springing up all along its banks. Then a few weeks later, after we had moved to Pittsburgh, one of the pastors from our church in Dallas stopped by our apartment on his way to Akron to give us a word from the Lord. "I believe I have a Scripture for you," he said. "It's Isaiah 43:18–21."

Then he read these words:

> "Do not call to mind the former things, or ponder things of the past. Behold, I will do something new, now it will spring forth; will you not be aware of it? I will even make a roadway in the wilderness, rivers in the desert."

He had not known about Bill's vision. The Scripture he had received confirmed what God had been speaking to us. It gave us hope.

From that time on we were encouraged when a number of guest speakers also prophesied about this "River." We kept a record of these prophecies. Some sounded grandiose, but we wrote them down anyway and I stuffed them into a manila envelope. Across the front of the envelope I wrote this verse: "And blessed is she who believed that there would be a fulfillment of what had been spoken to her by the Lord" (Luke 1:45).

Once in a while, we would read over the words of prophecy and even memorize some of them. They promised that a "River" would bring signs and wonders and we were to prepare for this season of blessing. Still, it seemed surreal. How could we prepare for something we did not understand? There was surely no visible sign that any of it would come to pass.

All of these experiences proved to be "stage-setting" on God's part. God was making both Bill and me tired, even sick of the ordinary, so that He might invade our lives with the extraordinary sense of His loving presence. Had we not been so completely disgusted with business as usual in the church and so desperately in need ourselves, we would have completely missed these years of outpouring of the Holy Spirit. God had done an excellent job of making us hungry for what He was about to give.

Here is how He satisfied the hunger He gave us.

The River Flows

Though Bill and I longed for revival, we probably did not have a full picture of what it really meant until it happened. Revival is not a whiff of inspiration or the goose bumps you feel when a great preacher preaches or a dynamic singer sings. It is not even a planned set of meetings set aside on the church calendar. Nor is revival a series of altar calls where people rush forward to accept Christ or join the church.

What we commonly call "revival" is a discernible sense of the Holy Spirit's presence that sovereignly descends on a local church and spreads to the world outside its walls. When revival comes, the spiritual heartbeat of the local church body quickens to a rapid rate. Suddenly fruit we could never produce through the most well-planned programs begins to form. The Holy Spirit opens spiritually blind eyes to see what only moments before was taken for granted.

As the spiritual eyes of the Church fly open, awe begins to pervade the congregation. As in the days of the early Church, the Holy Spirit continues to move. He might restore believ-

ers to a first-love passion for the Lord Jesus or draw unbelievers to the cross or display God's power in signs, wonders
and miracles. The presence of this awe separates what we
commonly call revival from business as usual. And once you
have tasted it, you will never be satisfied again without more
of Him. If you are honest, you will be forever unable to enjoy
its substitutes.

I first tasted this present revival in that dry, barren year of
1994. Bill and I had heard about an unusual outpouring of
the Holy Spirit on a church congregation in Toronto, Canada,
and decided to visit. I did not bring much with me in the way
of hope. My emotions were nearly dead, except for sadness.
I did not expect anything to happen. In fact, I could not. How
could I after nearly two decades of hope followed by repeated
disappointment?

At that time Toronto's meetings were held in an old shop-
ping center near the airport runway on Dixie Drive. As soon
as I walked through the front door I noticed something different in the atmosphere.

It was the Wednesday pastors' meeting and Guy Chevreau,
a Baptist theologian, was teaching about the historical and
biblical basis for revival, the difference between the old and
the new. His talk captured my attention, particularly what
he said about the Great Awakening. During that revival,
which occurred in New England in the 1700s, thirteen
unsuspecting communities woke up one morning to revival.
It had crept through small New England villages including
Northampton, Massachusetts, and into the parish of Jonathan
Edwards. They had not been fasting or praying for it or even
expecting it to happen.

Jonathan Edwards, a Congregational minister, had been
tired of the ordinary, too. He wrote in his essay, "A Narrative
of Surprising Conversions," these words: "Just after my
grandfather's death, it seemed to be a time of extraordinary
dullness in religion." Jonathan Edwards, who was to become
a famous eighteenth-century revival leader, had also been

disgusted with his powerlessness in the face of pervasive spiritual darkness.

Guy Chevreau went on to describe how during the course of the revival, Jonathan Edwards' own wife began to experience unusual manifestations such as "faintings," where her bodily strength would give way under the sense of "His nearness to me and my dearness to Him." It was as though her passion for her Lord was so ignited by a special sense of God's presence that had descended on their church that she often could not stand or perform her daily chores.

Guy's tone was disarming. There was no "hype" coming from the platform. I had attended far too many meetings in which the speakers used loud exhortations to stimulate an emotional response from their audiences; but this congregation did not need motivation. Although the meeting had not been formally advertised, some four hundred ministers from all over the world were present. The news had spread to them, as it had to us, by word of mouth. These people had come expecting to meet God, and their hunger was transforming the atmosphere into an altar for His presence.

My cynicism began to melt. How had all those people gotten there? What was it about the meeting that made some of the best speakers in the world, those who knew the Bible thoroughly, sit and listen to teaching about Church history?

As the lesson ended, Guy instructed everyone to stand, clear the folding chairs and move to the lines marked with duct tape on the carpet if they wanted to receive prayer. To my surprise no one left the meeting. Everyone stepped up to the lines. Then various individuals—not clergy, just "regular people"—began to walk down the lines praying for the ministers and their spouses one by one.

Suddenly the power level in the room seemed to escalate. As those who were praying lightly touched the people standing in the lines, those who were being prayed for fell back as though acted upon by an invisible force. Some broke out in uproarious laughter; some were shaking violently; others began to sob uncontrollably. The unseen presence of the Lord began to envelop them, and those who fell remained on the floor as though they could not absorb enough of the experience.

Then Guy came to Bill and me. "What are your names?" he asked gently.

"We're the Fishes. And we're really dry," I replied.

Of all the prayers Guy could have prayed, he prayed this one: "Well, then, let the River flow."

Suddenly the River we had been prophetically promised for eighteen years began to trickle into our dry souls. It came up from within and also from without. Bill and I did not fall; we cried. I had not cried in church in years. Nothing moved me until now, but as the tears flowed I began to feel hope inside.

Throughout the weekend we focused our attention on what some were daring to call revival. After each service we stood to receive prayer, even though I was actually hesitant to receive prayer another time for fear nothing would happen. I was wrong. The refreshing sense of the presence of God deepened. All around we noticed the outward signs of people writhing under the influence of the Holy Spirit as though despair was being sucked out of them.

The next night a man on the prayer team named Ron Dick approached my husband, my son and me as we stood waiting for prayer. "May I pray for you?" he asked smiling.

"Certainly," I said.

"Come, Holy Spirit," he prayed confidently. This time the Holy Spirit came as a gentle, but firm pressure against my chest. No one was touching me. In that moment I had a choice. I could either yield to the Holy Spirit or resist Him. I could get in this long-awaited River or refuse it. I decided to yield.

In the next moment I was looking up at the ceiling in an envelope of the presence of God. I saw in my mind's eye a vision of Jesus laughing over me as though He knew what was about to happen. I did not want to move. I only wanted the moment never to end. I was touching an eternal realm, a dimension I knew I was being prepared to inherit, and I did not want to disturb whatever it was that God was doing.

This was the moment revival began for me. Many Christians can remember the moment when the conviction of the Holy Spirit collided with their human wills and surrender gave way to new birth. I cannot, but I can remember that moment. I will never forget it.

It was the first of thousands of divine moments as revival invaded our ordinary lives.

THE FIREFALL

Today, when I get out of my car in the parking lot of Toronto Airport Christian Fellowship, even after more than 45 visits to its former and current locations, I can sense the presence of God. Renewal and revival continue from the day—January 20, 1994—when the Holy Spirit fell on that tiny church.

From that small beginning a major outpouring of the Holy Spirit has erupted. What some have called "the Toronto Blessing" has spread to the Body of Christ on every continent of the world and ignited other fires, including "the Pensacola (Fla.) Outpouring." In fact, since the outpouring began, more than three and one-half million people, including more than three hundred thousand pastors, have made their way to Toronto seeking a touch from God in their own lives and for their churches.

Toronto traces its own roots to the outpouring of the Holy Spirit in Argentina, evidence that the torch is passing throughout the world. More precious than any man-generated Olympic flame, the fire the Holy Spirit ignites is a treasure from God. Like the Israelite priests looking after the fire on the altar of the Temple, God is calling leaders in the Church to keep and tend this fire of revival.

Tragically, however, many in the Church have ignored and rejected the outpouring. Perhaps even sadder, in many places the outpouring began only to dissipate as leaders let go of the long-awaited blessing. But in churches of every size throughout the world, many have clung to the revival and are seeing a new dimension of the Holy Spirit take up residence and continue to produce supernatural fruit.

The River is swarming with a harvest of fish, a multitude of lost people finding their heavenly Father for the first time. The Holy Spirit is renewing the first-love passion for Jesus in once apathetic Christians, causing them to want to lay down their lives for Him. He is turning tired local churches into watering holes of revival in their regions. He is resurrecting nearly dead ministries and giving them new fervor. So how long will it last?

In this book, I want to dispel forever the myth that revival blessing is only meant to be temporary. We will talk about how we can make a comfortable hearth for the Holy Spirit's fire so that He will not only come but stay. We will meet some of the unlikely people who have been touched and some of the churches, large and small, that have been ignited by this fire. We will also take a hard look at what quenches revival so that we can adjust our lives to facilitate this new move of God.

While much of the Church is fasting and praying for revival, maybe we need to ask some questions. Is revival already here and I am not aware of it? Am I ready to treasure the cherished blessing when it breaks out in my church and in my own life? Is it possible to keep revival?

Let us begin our search for answers by looking at what I call "the revival equation."

Two

The Revival Equation

What Bill and I did not realize during our first trip to Toronto was that we had become part of the "revival equation." When desperation collides with supernatural visitation, it equals a download of revival into your life—whether you like it or not!

Let's look at two examples of this equation, the first focusing on spiritual hunger and the second on contact with a supernatural God. We will then see some surprising elements that do *not* belong in the equation.

Spiritual Hunger

Reports continue to circulate of congregations all over the world receiving supernatural visitations after their pastors or leaders made a trip to a site of outpouring such as Toronto or Pensacola. One of them is a Foursquare Gospel Church pastor from Fresno, California, named Brad Davis, who was hungry for a work of God.

In fact, when Brad Davis arrived in Toronto in October 1994 he was famished. He and his wife, Cathy, had been church planting in Fresno for nine years. Hungry to start a church, they had left a prestigious position as youth ministers at The Church On The Way in Van Nuys, California, and had gone to work. By the time 1994 came, their congregation numbered 120 people, but that was all you could say about it.

"We had it so well-timed that you could get the service over with, have the equipment put away and be home before the game started," Brad recalls. One day as Brad was listening to a baseball game on the radio, a batter for his team hit a grand slam. Brad leapt out of his living room chair cheering. Suddenly, the inner conviction of the Holy Spirit came to him and he found himself wondering, *Lord Jesus, why am I not that excited about You anymore?*

Brad began to pray about this, but it seemed that the more he prayed the worse things got. People were leaving the church looking for spiritually higher ground. One day as Brad was praying, he heard the Lord say to him, *I'm going to give your congregation a new heart.*

Shortly afterward, a young man in their church had a heart attack. Brad went to the hospital to pray for him. The following Sunday the man testified before the church that the doctor said, "It's as though you have been given a new heart." Brad saw the young man's healing and his doctor's response as a confirmation to the word he had received from God, but he soon learned that the congregation did not share his enthusiasm. The news seemed to sail right over their heads. They could not hear it, at least not with spiritual ears.

Brad was waking up to the horror that many pastors in Western countries face, the fear that we are living like the Laodicean church mentioned in Revelation 3. That church was so rich it had need of nothing but missed the truth that it was really wretched, miserable, poor, blind and naked. Worse yet, there seems to be no way to motivate such a church out of its death spiral. The only thing left to do is go through religious motions and pray that if Jesus knocks on the door, as He did with Laodicea, we will respond.

In the summer of 1994, Brad and Cathy began to hear about the outbreak of the Holy Spirit in Toronto. On the outside chance that it might be God, Brad decided to go out on a limb, purchase a ticket to Toronto's first Catch the Fire Conference in October of that year and go there himself to see firsthand.

When Brad arrived, he began to feel the presence of God that hovers over Toronto to this day as the revival fires continue to burn brightly. Brad called Cathy in tears. "Hon', God is here," Brad kept saying.

At first Cathy thought Brad was having a nervous breakdown, but when he returned home she found that she had a new husband. They could not wait until Sunday to see what would happen at the service. They were not disappointed. The presence of God fell upon the congregation and their sleeping church woke up. Today, the Father's House in Fresno, California, is like a spring in the desert where the thirsty can continually access the presence of God.

Signs of a Ripe Harvest

Many other people like Brad and Cathy who treasure what God is doing also have in common this desperation for His presence, which is itself a sign of the Holy Spirit's work. I love how the Living Bible translates Matthew 5:3: "God blesses those who realize their need for Him, for the Kingdom of Heaven is given to them." Until people perceive their own need, there is no use trying to fill it.

The general lack of hunger in the Western church is in sharp contrast to what you find in developing nations where people know several dimensions of desperation. Their spiritual hunger is so intense it feels as if they vacuum the blessing right out of those who are privileged to carry it to them.

In the Ukraine, the former breadbasket of the Soviet Union, missionary Dan Slade functions like a modern-day Philip. Hoping to light fires of revival in the country, he arranges conferences in the Ukraine's major cities. At Dan's invitation, Bill and I traveled more than nine thousand miles to help Dan and his teams carry the blessing to this country.

We were devastated by what we saw. What should have been a first-world nation is in ruins. The Communist government, following on the heels of the czars, quenched creative competition and all hope in this generation of a better life. Existence there is bleak as it regresses into a third-world nation and divides into two classes of people. Concrete highrises are crumbling amid weeds. Women work large fields with hand implements. Trilingual people cannot get jobs. Daily, people who have no hope throw themselves under trains to end their miserable lives.

But the nation is in spiritual harvest. Bill and I spoke at a church in the heart of Kiev to a congregation of more than fifteen hundred people packed into a civic auditorium for Wednesday night prayer meeting. They had not been told to expect guest speakers; they were just hungry to be there. When I asked the audience how many had been saved in the past ten years, about 98 percent of the hands went up, indicating that since the downfall of the Communist regime the Holy Spirit has descended on that nation with ardent fervor.

As the Holy Spirit's laughter broke out on people in the congregation at that conference in Kiev, most of the people leaned forward in their seats, amazed at what God was doing. People came forward for prayer and for salvation. Healing signs and wonders uncommon in meetings in North America happened in every service.

Missionaries there confess to finding it easy to give up all the comforts of the West just to be in a place where there is such hunger for God. After ministering in the Ukraine, I realized that I had spent most of my life in ministry, especially prior to this outpouring of the Holy Spirit, trying to feed people who were not truly hungry for what I had to give. Spiritual appetite like this is a gift from God, part of His revival that we must recognize and treasure.

When Moses spoke his last words to Israel before his death and before they entered the Promised Land, he reminded them of the way God had brought them. He said:

> "You shall remember all the way which the LORD your God has led you in the wilderness these forty years, that He might humble you, testing you, to know what was in your heart, whether you would keep His commandments or not. He humbled you and let you be hungry, and fed you with manna which you did not know, nor did your fathers know, that He might make you understand that man does not live by bread alone, but man lives by everything that proceeds out of the mouth of the LORD."
>
> Deuteronomy 8:2–3

Prior to the advent of revival, God prepares His people by creating in them a hunger that will be satisfied only by the sweetness of the "manna" He sends, which is His own presence, a greater dimension of the Holy Spirit. I remember one minister saying, "God doesn't send revival, He comes Himself." Spiritual hunger causes the Christian to be able to discern between that which is supernaturally satisfying and that which is not. He creates a taste for Himself. Unbelievers who experience this God-given spiritual hunger often testify to having tried all sorts of strange doctrines looking for the right "taste" that satisfies. When Jesus touches their spiritual palates, they are forever sated.

For the hungry person, the table setting does not really matter. The outward signs do not offend and keep them away from the banquet. The supernaturally created hunger in them is enough to overcome pride, fear and everything else that stands in the way of partaking of what God is graciously setting before them. And their eager response delights the heart of God.

Spiritual hunger comes to individuals and congregations. Before the current outpouring broke over our congregation, I often wished that Bill and I had a bigger church and even different faces to preach to every week, people I thought would be more eager to receive. But when the outpouring started, I quickly saw the wisdom of God's handiwork. Practically every person who had been drawn to be a part of our congregation was there because he or she was spiritually hungry for the presence of God. They responded to the revival like beggars to a banquet. Even a number of people who had recently left the congregation found their way back home to the table.

SIGNS OF SPIRITUAL HUNGER

How do I know if I am spiritually hungry? That is, how do I know if I am spiritually hungry for the things of God?

Spiritual hunger, as we have seen, causes you to feel hungry for the presence of God and at the same time full of what He has already given you. But there is another kind of spiritual hunger, one that has a devastating effect. In the spiritual, as with the physical, anyone who goes long enough without eating ultimately loses the sense of hunger pangs. The spiritual "digestive tract" gradually goes to sleep and you no longer feel hungry. Unless the process is interrupted, you will starve.

The danger with this form of spiritual hunger is that once you lose all desire to eat, when nourishment comes you will regurgitate it. Spiritually starving people often do not know they are starving. They are missing the nourishment that comes from close contact with a supernatural God who imparts life, and yet they do not know what to do about it. As much as a physically starving child's belly looks swollen and his extremities pencil-thin, so the spiritually starving individual is weak and held up by no more than fragile sticks of perseverance.

If you recognize this in yourself, realize that there is no need to stay that way. You are living in a day when God is setting out a lavish feast of spiritual nourishment to fulfill the desire for Him that He has created in you. What you need now is the next component of the revival equation: contact with a supernatural God.

CONTACT WITH A SUPERNATURAL GOD

Sometimes, as with Brad and Cathy Davis, it takes a spark to ignite the fires of revival.

Sometimes, though, fires ignite from spontaneous combustion. In the material world, unseen components of a chemical equation come together and suddenly, without warning, fire starts. Similarly, in the spiritual world some revivals begin without any apparent contact with other revivals.

Bill and I have ministered in more than one church in North America that saw the earmarks of the current move of God before it broke out in Toronto. The Holy Spirit seemed to fall on the congregations without warning, as He did at Pentecost.

But something happened in Toronto that changed Church history forever. In the paradigm described by Malcolm Gladwell, author of *The Tipping Point: How Little Things Make a Big Difference* (Little, Brown & Co., 2000), Toronto's meetings "tipped." In other words several factors came together at a critical moment to cause a snowball effect: Meetings escalated rapidly in size and the news spread all over the world. A main factor was the Holy Spirit's choice of Toronto as a meeting place. (It is interesting that in the First Nation language, *Toronto* means "meeting place.")

Gladwell makes a parallel point with the revivals of Wesley and Whitfield. Although the two evangelists were contemporaries and friends, and although Whitfield was reportedly a better speaker, Wesley's meetings "tipped" and Whitfield's did not. Although Whitfield gathered large crowds, the snowball effect never happened, at least not to the same degree that it did with Wesley.

Similarly, Rodney Howard-Browne held powerful meetings in the summer of 1993 and into 1994 at Carpenter's Home Church in Florida. He attracted thousands, but those meetings never "tipped" as did the ones in Toronto.

Let me state here that if you are seeking revival, be careful not to confuse a revival's "tipping point" with the revival itself, which is the presence of God. While there may be only a few places that "tip," I believe that any heart and any church willing to accommodate Him can have His reviving, renewing presence, as we will see later in this book.

Let's take a moment for a brief look at the "spontaneous combustion" experience at Toronto, when our supernatural God made contact with His hungering people.

What Happened in Toronto

On January 20, 1994, Randy Clark, a pastor from St. Louis, traveled with a team from his church to Toronto. The request came from John Arnott, senior pastor of the church now known as Toronto Airport Christian Fellowship. John and his wife, Carol, had made a trip to Argentina in November 1993, which left them desperately hungry for God. John had heard that God had touched Randy powerfully in the meetings of evangelist Rodney Howard-Browne and that Randy was now carrying a new anointing. John wanted the blessing, too.

As Randy began the meetings, the Holy Spirit came in power. In John Arnott's words, "The level of anointing in the room suddenly rose and people's love for Jesus went off the scale." People were laughing, falling, shaking and crying.

John called a group of pastors together the next day to receive prayer. After the Holy Spirit touched them, news began to spread by word of mouth throughout southern Ontario. Word continued to spread and now, as I have stated, people come to the Fellowship from all over the world.

God seems to have, in the words of our pastor friend David Matthews, "localized" Himself in a place where the hungry and thirsty could get to Him. In computer terminology, by making a pilgrimage to Toronto we can "access" the tangible presence of God and "download" it into our lives. Throughout the ages, pilgrimages are one way that people seek God; as with the wise men's sojourn to Bethlehem, people find God by hearing that He is touchable somewhere and going there.

From Toronto to Pensacola

Among the hungry seekers at Toronto's nightly renewal meetings in March 1995 was a pastor's wife from a large Assembly of God church in the Florida panhandle. Brenda Kilpatrick was living through a period of discouragement, too. Her mother-in-law was ill and near death, and Brenda was wrestling with periods of hopelessness.

When Brenda stood on one of the lines to receive prayer in Toronto, she began to encounter a supernatural God who loved her. She found herself "glued" to the floor. Her experiences there moved her from skepticism to deeper faith, and they also left a deposit of the love of Jesus.

When she returned home, she found herself intermittently immobilized under the weight of God's glory. Over a period of several weeks, God made her a sign and a wonder to her husband, John, who himself was at a low point in his personal life and ministry. The Holy Spirit had been stirring him to want more. He finally said, "I know your life, Brenda. Because of what God is doing with you, I know He will bring revival to our church."

Within weeks the now famous Father's Day Outpouring fell in the Sunday morning service of Brownsville Assembly of God in Pensacola. Evangelist Steve Hill was preaching that day. John Kilpatrick's mother had recently died, and John had asked Steve to come and hold meetings at his church. Steve's own fire was lit at Holy Trinity, Brompton, an Anglican church in the heart of London that had been renewed by the Toronto Blessing.

As Steve ministered to those responding to the altar call, John Kilpatrick suddenly fell backward on the platform and was immobilized himself for several hours. He and his wife finally had to be helped from the building.

The congregation rushed forward. Within days the meetings there "tipped" and Pensacola became a site of outpouring. First people from all over the American South began to come; then it spread to other states and then foreign countries. Three million or more people have journeyed to Pensacola to receive a touch from God. Hundreds of thousands have been saved; backsliders have returned; healings abound; and thousands more have received the baptism of the Holy Spirit and the renewal blessings as well.

Thus, after observing the spread of revival for some years, I have seen the equation at work many times: Desperate hunger for God coupled with the supernatural dimension of His presence will lead to personal experience of the blessing. Whether the fire starts from a spark or from spontaneous combustion, any time the conditions are right fire will ignite and spread. As the flame reaches more "dry wood," which always burns faster, revival blazes.

I recall with laughter a scene on a British television program at the time of the last summer Olympics: Someone decked out in scuba gear was carrying the Olympic torch underwater. If ever an image describes the spread of revival, this is it! Fire in the River carried by one person to another from one nation to another.

Is Something Left Out of the Equation?

Students of revival will notice that I have left out of the equation several factors that others stress. So often I have read that "fasting + prayer + unity = revival." Others argue that church size is a factor. And a number of pastors focus on repentance as a prerequisite. Are these facets of church life important to revival?

Fasting, Prayer and Unity: Isn't This the Place to Start?

What about "fasting + prayer + unity"? Is this an accurate formula for revival? Actually, no. As we look at Church history we see that these components, as important as they are, do not bring revival. Those who have fasted and prayed fervently for revival only to see it elude their grasps understand that this notion is false.

Rather, as I have already suggested, the prayer and fasting that seem to result in revival are its byproducts, not its causes. This was certainly the case with the Brownsville Assembly of God, as the Lord had been stirring the congregation to pray every Sunday night for revival. Effective prayer and fasting are all but impossible unless the Holy Spirit inspires them. As part of a season of renewal they are also part of the revival itself. Maybe I am touching a sacred cow, but we need to examine the truth.

In the '80s, I fully explored the religious treadmill of trying to generate revival by human effort. The shame of not having it or the guilt for not wanting it can drive the performance-oriented, sincere Christian to hope that greater spiritual disciplines will bring results. But the bottom line is still a hunger that is more often experienced as emptiness for His presence.

How this hunger manifests itself in outward disciplines is different for every person. In fact, most of the pastors I know who are experiencing revival in their churches today had given up praying and fasting for revival years before the outpouring came. Many of them had fervently prayed and fasted years before only to realize that it was not God's season to move. Others were praying out of duty, hoping against hope that they would press the right button and revival would fall. They were surprised when God came, often years later.

As I mentioned above, I believe that the prayer many people believe prefaces a revival is really a part of the revival itself. In the first stages of an outpouring, God gives people who are normally not motivated to pray the grace-motivated hunger to do so. Prayers that once were halfhearted take on new fervency and that fervency is not self-motivated.

In fact, I wonder if the early believers were praying the moment the Holy Spirit fell at Pentecost, because the Bible says that the sound of the rushing wind filled the whole house where they were "sitting." In biblical times Jewish people generally prayed while standing up, not sitting down.

And what about all the times when others equally loved by God and faithful to Him prayed and fasted for revival and it never came? I love what John Arnott says when people ask him why God moved in Toronto. He shrugs and suggests, "Because it's near the airport?" He does not take credit for being hungrier or more faithful than anyone else in his pursuit of God.

And just as prayer and fasting are not prerequisites for revival, neither is community-wide unity. Church history never records a sustained outpouring that was prefaced by community-wide unity. A basic level of cooperation is necessary to hold a big event, but this is different from a God-initiated outpouring of His presence.

The insinuation that unity precedes revival—that we must get everyone together and in one accord in order to see God move—is based on revisionist history. The outpouring itself brings unity as the Holy Spirit bonds people together through common experience and a common language that describes the way God is moving. We will look at this in more depth in chapter 7.

But what about Pentecost? Were they not all in one accord? Pentecost involved about a hundred and twenty people, the size of a small local church today. These were all who were left in Jerusalem of the more than five hundred who had seen Jesus ascend into heaven. This gives everyone hope.

Doesn't Church Size Matter?

Recently Bill and I visited Moriah Chapel in Lukor, Wales, the site of the beginning of the Welsh Revival in 1904. It began one night when Evan Roberts, the newly appointed youth minister, asked everyone to leave who wanted to and then locked the door on the small group of young people who remained. As they sat on the wooden benches in the fellowship hall, the same benches that are there today, the Holy Spirit fell upon them. Within two years more than one hundred thousand people had been saved.

This should be enough to encourage us that church size does not have anything to do with where revival falls either. While it may come to a large multi-thousand-member congregation like Brownsville Assembly of God in Pensacola, it could just as well show up in a tiny congregation where the hearts are open. The fact that Jesus was born in Bethlehem is enough to give anyone hope that God will come to humble circumstances.

Our friend Tino DiSienna, a pastor in Queens, New York, was in prayer one day facing a conflict. He wanted God to come in power but he was afraid because his church did not have a parking lot, a big congregation or a number of things many people say you must have in order for God to move. God spoke to Tino, probably in a New York City accent, and said, "I don't need a runway to land."

God is moving in congregations of all sizes. We are all part of one big Church from God's point of view. John Arnott said to me one day, "It's the little churches that are really going for it." Perhaps this is because a smaller church is more easily focused than a crowd of several thousand with hundreds of groups distracted by different concerns.

Isn't Repentance Vital?

Revival literature of the nineteenth and twentieth centuries usually stressed the need for repentance on the part of those praying for revival. This has caused earnest seekers of revival to hunt for the personal or corporate sin that seems to be holding back the cherished blessing. I have often heard messages from well-meaning preachers indicating that those desiring revival must let God know they mean business by repenting.

So, seekers cling to a man-generated repentance that, in its desperate search for cleansing, actually resembles obsessive-compulsive behavior. It is motivated by ungodly fear, not conviction of the Holy Spirit, and does not result in permanent change.

Others choose performance-oriented behaviors like fasting for long periods and intense calling out to God to show hearts of repentance. It gives the impression that the Lord is waiting to see a perfect performance before He will send revival.

Scriptural precedents are quite different. After the Holy Spirit fell at Pentecost, Peter told the crowd of sinners to repent, knowing that the One who convicts of sin was now there to save. On another occasion he told Simon the magician that repentance is a gift from God (see Acts 8). He told him to pray for the gift of repentance that leads to life.

When God begins to grant wide-scale repentance—where people come running back to God, hungry for Him and longing to be touched by Him and to give themselves to Him wholeheartedly—revival has already begun. A close examination of Church history shows that revival comes to those who are far away from God in order to bring them back to the Father's arms.

The No-Formula Formula

The blessing of revival is not earned or deserved through human goodness or spiritual effort. It is not that easy. If it were, many of us would have had it years ago. We could have it anytime we wanted, and we would have proudly taken credit for it. Real revival has God's sovereign thumbprint on it. It is not obtained by following a prescribed formula. Our years of fruitless fasting, praying and repenting for it to come should remind us that we had nothing to do with it.

Consider this: Is it right to take the credit for an outpouring as though our discipline brought it? When God shows up in one place, it is likely because of the cumulative longing of hearts all over the world and the longing of God the Father for intimate communion with them, plus the fact that "the fullness of time" has come.

In that moment the Holy Spirit comes where He is needed, where the people are often weak from hungering for Him. And He flourishes in the congregation and in the heart that makes room for Him.

In our case, our church has not been a place where revival tipped and where thousands have been saved. Our congregation, like thousands of others all over the world, was hungry but did not know we needed what had been going on in Toronto. We just went there, and because God is faithful and because it was time for Him to begin fulfilling His words to us, we have become part of what all of us want to call the blessing of a lifetime.

After years of desperate dryness, the River came, and the River is still here.

Three

The River Hits the Church

When Guy Chevreau prayed for Bill and me that day in Toronto, "Let the River flow," he did not know what he was saying to us. He had prayed for thousands of people in 1994; he had no idea that the word *River* was a key for us that would unlock the door to all that God is doing. The sense of expectation that came to me in Toronto had been impossible to generate the week before. Within days signs of life broke out in the church we pastor.

The following Wednesday night Bill called everyone in the church together, and we shared our experiences in Toronto. Bill's experience, as you will see in a moment, was very different from mine. People asked all sorts of questions about how this would affect us, but Bill had to reply honestly, "I don't know." Then at the next service Bill started praying for people and all the signs people commonly see in Toronto began to happen to people who had never seen them before. People began to cry, laugh, tremble and fall.

They say in Toronto that both individuals and churches should continually receive prayer because the presence of God will increase; we took them at their word. We asked the Holy Spirit to come at the beginning of every meeting we held. Since 1994 we have never failed to end a service with personal ministry where we ask the Holy Spirit to come upon anyone who wants to receive more of God's love, and He has come every time. The outward manifestations still happen and the inward sense of the love of God continues to flow into everyone who receives it, with amazing effects in their lives.

MAKE A PLACE FOR ME

God's presence has an innocent, almost childlike quality to it. Back then, we did not realize that He wanted to be part of literally everything we were doing. When He showed up, He needed center stage. We did not know exactly what would happen when we got together. People who had been apathetic about coming to church suddenly scrambled to get there because they were in awe of what God was doing. The Holy Spirit was coming upon everyone who wanted Him, His power often producing violent effects.

We did not mind the outward signs; we had begun feasting on a dimension of the presence of God and they simply happened. One person would be lying on the carpet weeping while a person a few feet away could not seem to stop laughing. Regardless of the outward effects, the River of God's presence refreshed everyone who touched it. Even today the sounds of those receiving prayer are like those of people swimming in a watering hole on a very hot day. People just enjoy God, and it creates a joyful noise.

As the months passed, the Holy Spirit remained. We soon realized that even if a service did not go so well, He would not leave. Even at our personal worst moments, He stayed. It seemed impossible to grieve Him away except by ignoring Him and not wanting Him anymore. He was patient with us in our sins.

Nearly eleven years before on a Sunday night when our church was still located in the inner city, a prophetic song started welling up within me: "Make a place for Me, and I will dwell in the midst of Thee, if you make a place for Me. . . ." That was back when we prophesied in King James English with words like *midst* and *Thee*, but we got the message anyway. At some point, God would be coming and He wanted us to prepare a place for Him.

When the Holy Spirit started coming with this new outpouring, we finally understood what He had been talking about. We needed to make a place for Him in our services. A central place. The most important place. He wanted more than dead air space after the worship songs so that a few people could prophesy. He wanted to radically change what we were doing. Our small measure of effectiveness was far from the abundance of fruit He could produce if we would make a place for Him.

This involved inward and outward changes, not the least of which was seeing the pastor himself radically affected. Here in his own words is Bill's view of what was happening to him.

> After the Holy Spirit had been breaking out in our church for three months, Melinda and Beverly Watt, now our associate pastor, went to Toronto again to take a closer look at what God is doing. When they returned, they were full of even greater expectation believing this might be the long-awaited outpouring of the Holy Spirit.
>
> I was happy to hear their testimonies, but to tell you the truth they provoked me. From my first exposure to this on our first trip to Toronto I could not receive anything. When I prayed for people, everyone seemed to be

receiving but me. In Toronto, it seemed that I was the only one who was left standing the first time. I think John Arnott himself must have seen my plight and prayed for me five times. The last time he prayed I was still standing, and I thought I heard him tell his catcher quietly, "Well, we do the best we can."

When Beverly and Melinda came back from their trip to Toronto, my frustration had reached its peak. I could not stand it anymore. After their testimonies in one of our services about what God was continuing to pour out in Toronto, they invited those who wanted to receive another dose of His presence to come forward for more prayer.

I decided to be the first one in line. I was not going to pray for another person until God touched me. When Beverly and Melinda prayed for me that day, I began to feel a slight pressure as though I needed to yield to God. I decided not to resist anymore. Honestly, I had begun to pride myself on being the only one in a prayer line left standing because I did not really believe there was much to this falling business. I had seen too many people whose lives were not changed even after falling under the power. The next thing I knew I had yielded to the slightest sense of the presence of God. Now I was on the floor.

Suddenly I felt the presence of Jesus next to me. Everyone had been hearing such wonderful words from God. I could not wait to hear what He was going to say to me now that He had me on the floor.

Then I thought I heard Him say, *You're a wild donkey of a man!* His tone was full of humor. Instead of feeling insulted, I felt known. God who knew me and loved me was beginning a new work in my heart.

I had been brought up in an Air Force family, the son of a military officer. We had placed little value on emotional expressions, perhaps because we had to brace ourselves for the inevitable changes in location and relationships that came every two or three years with new orders. I have never been emotionally exuberant. In fact, like many men, I did not think about feeling anything about anything. I did not know how badly I needed to feel something in order to flow in this River.

Since that day, God has made me into a continual seeker and soaker. I receive prayer at every service and often ask the prayer team to pray for me. As I keep soaking, the Lord keeps changing my heart, and He keeps giving the congregation a new pastor.

When my husband fell on the floor that day, anyone who had any doubt in our congregation about the moving of the Spirit put it aside. People almost could not believe it. If this pastor could be touched, God could do anything. My husband was always composed and his emotional responses stayed reserved even in very extreme situations; he was the model of decorum at serious events like weddings and funerals; plus he looks great in a suit!

When Bill started letting God touch him, it gave everyone permission to relax and receive, too. In fact, we have noticed since then that the congregations that hold onto the blessing are those in which the pastor continues to receive. God is not calling leaders these days to administrate or oversee without continually receiving His touch themselves. If they choose not to, they will inevitably make decisions that quench the Holy Spirit.

More Change

Once my husband began to experience the Father's love, He knew it was to die for. He started to make any change necessary to accommodate the blessing, and in spite of some protests from ladies of the church, he started with the antique oak pews. Everyone was falling to the floor in response to prayer, and we did not have room at the front and in the aisles to accommodate those who wanted to rest in the presence of God, sometimes for an hour at a time.

Our church owns a Gothic-style building on a neighbor-hood street corner in Trafford, Pennsylvania, a town in the east suburbs of Pittsburgh. It was built in the 1920s with breathtaking stained glass windows and beautiful dark oak pews. However, denominational church design in the '20s was never meant to accommodate revival. There was not enough space both to pray and have room for all the people falling and soaking in God's presence.

At that time Bill and I lived next door in the parsonage, which is separated by a common wall, and I can remember the sound of tapping coming from the church as Bill pried up the bolts holding the pews to the floor. Each week another pew disappeared until almost all of them were stored away.

We ran an ad in the paper not realizing how much in demand they were. The income from the sale along with other donations we had received gave us enough money to buy new carpet. This was an outward sign, almost prophetic in nature, of our church's inner desire to get rid of anything, even valuable, traditional things, that stood in the way of the Holy Spirit's moving.

Another change from the old was the way we worshipped. The new songs being sung in Toronto seemed to carry a sound that moved us. Every revival produces fresh songs. When people sing those songs it is a sign that they are laying aside the old and becoming part of the new thing He is doing. We had been singing meaningful worship songs for years but these were different. The new sound carried an unusual anointing that made people listen and open up to God. We started to sing the songs and noticed an even stronger man-ifestation of God's presence anointing the worship.

Gradually, Paul Blackham, who had helped Bill for years with the worship, moved into position of worship leader. As Paul soaked in God's presence, God began to give him new songs, too. These also carry the sound that comes from being born out of the move of the Holy Spirit. One of them, nick-named "The Be-Be Song," was featured on Toronto's "Celebration" CD and has gone all over the world. Paul has now produced two CDs featuring some of the songs that have come to him as he soaks in God's presence.

As with removing the pews, changing the worship music to accommodate the new move of the Holy Spirit did not initially please everyone, but the sound continues to draw the hungry to the outpouring of the Holy Spirit.

More changes were to come. Next we reexamined our church activities. Had we generated the program or activity to draw people or to accommodate God's presence? If it was created for the wrong reason we got rid of it, even if it looked as though it produced fruit. We only knew that God wanted to touch everyone with His love. Anything we had to do to make way for the people to receive, we did.

We called everyone into the services to receive what God was pouring out, even the children—except for the tiniest ones. Nancy Westerberg, the children's pastor, taught the children about what we were experiencing and then brought them into the sanctuary for prayer. Today little children, teenagers and young adults all receive prayer alongside the oldest members of the congregation.

We even took a long hard look at the church "dress code." Bill hates suits and had griped every Sunday morning about putting one on. When he saw revival taking place in Toronto with casual dress, he felt he had permission to let go of what we have often jokingly called a prophetic symbol of rigid control, the tie.

One Sunday morning he turned to the worship team, pulled off his tie and has not worn one in our regular services since. To our surprise, the Holy Spirit did not leave. Instead, people began to relax and receive His presence more readily, feeling perhaps as though God accepted them in their normal state.

In the beginning a lot of honest and heartfelt questions arose about the unusual things that were happening. Bill and I laid a foundation by teaching about scriptural evidence for what God is doing, and we circulated Guy Chevreau's tapes on revival history. This gave a safe footing for those who were sincere but unsure about our new focus.

We have never pressured or intimidated our parishioners into receiving prayer. We let them come to God as He draws them. Most, however, are prompted to receive prayer by one other change they see: the change in people's lives.

Here is an example.

"Sober in the Spirit"

The Holy Spirit had been moving in the congregation for several months when our children's pastor, Nancy Westerberg, planned to testify. She wanted to tell how God had been moving in her life since the day the Holy Spirit instantly lifted a three-year depression from her shoulders. She fell under the power, then jumped up from the floor and began to dance me around the sanctuary. She was completely different. Before, she had been plagued with depression, and when it lifted, despair and hopelessness left, too.

Nancy had watched from her childhood as alcoholism ravaged and killed too many members of her family. Now it was working on her son, Bill. As a teen Bill had been a part of our congregation and on the worship team. He had even begun attending Bible college. One day, however, depression took over and he took a drink. He could not stop. One led to another and for nearly nine years he was a hopeless alcoholic.

Bill was able to hold down his printing job, but he spent much of his off time frequenting bars and drinking at home. Bill had attended Alcoholics Anonymous meetings many times and had experienced short stints of sobriety, but alcoholism had him and would not let go. We saw Bill from time to time and invited him back to church. He felt too full of shame to come. He sank further and further into a depressive spiral of shame and guilt followed by alcohol followed by more remorse.

On the Sunday his mother was going to testify, Bill came, and at the end of the service he received prayer. It seemed as though nothing happened and once again Bill went away disappointed.

Two weeks went by and on a Saturday morning our phone rang. Bill was on the other end of the line. It was clear that he had been drinking, and it was depressing him further as it usually did. His voice was sullen, but he was reaching out for the first time in years.

He asked sincerely, "Do you think now would be the time in my life when all my prophecies might start coming to pass?"

He said that ever since he had received prayer on that recent Sunday morning he had not been able to get out of his mind all the things God had promised him in the years he was walking with the Lord.

Suddenly, I started laughing. It was as though God was laughing in the face of the enemy that had controlled Bill for years. "Bill, your number is up!" I said with renewed confidence. "The Lord is after you, and He's not going to let go this time."

After a while Bill seemed a little more cheerful, and we said goodbye.

That evening the phone rang again and a different Bill was on the other end of the phone. This is what happened.

Bill said that after he hung up the first time he said to himself, *Well, if I'm going to go back to church and this is my last day to drink, I'm going to do it up right.* For a few hours he sat in his apartment drinking one glass after another.

Suddenly, at four o'clock in the afternoon the Holy Spirit fell on Bill in his apartment while he was alone. Bill started laughing and could not stop. He laughed so hard and so loudly that he was afraid his sister in the apartment below would hear him. He tried to hide his head under the sofa to muffle the sound.

Sure enough, his sister came running up the stairs. "Bill, what's wrong with you?" she asked. Noticing the near-empty bottle nearby she said, "I'm calling an ambulance. I'm sending you to detox. You're drunk."

Through the laughter, Bill managed to say, "Don't call the ambulance. There's nothing wrong with me. For the first time in years, I feel the love of Jesus all over me." When the Holy Spirit finally lifted His hand enough for Bill to collect himself, he was sober. The same Holy Spirit that was making everyone else "drunk in the Spirit" had the opposite effect on him.

When Bill called to tell us what had happened, he asked if he could come back to church. We were thrilled and awestruck, but we wondered if the change would last. I had written books about alcoholism and its horrible effects on families, and I knew what it took for most alcoholics to get sober. Would this be Bill's turning point?

Bill started coming to every meeting and always to the altar for prayer. He would fall under the power of the Holy Spirit and as the presence of God overtook him, he would laugh and enjoy himself and grow in intimacy with God. But one day, the urge to drink returned and Bill slipped. This time, however, instead of running away from God in despair, Bill ran to the Lord. He came to receive prayer and the Holy Spirit touched him again.

For several weeks the battle raged. Bill would get filled with the Holy Spirit and so inebriated with God's love that he could not stand up straight, only to have a struggle within the next few days. Inside, though, Bill had the gradually increasing hope that his addiction would leave him forever. Finally, the Holy Spirit won. Bill took one too many drinks of God's "new wine."

At this writing I am happy to report that Bill Westerberg has not had a drink in six years. He also quit smoking. He married Candi, a lovely woman in the congregation who is also being powerfully touched by the presence of God. Bill is back on the worship team, playing lead guitar and helping the worship leader produce CDs. His boss thinks so highly of him now that he recently promoted Bill to a managerial position.

Bill has traveled with us to prisons to spread the fire. In spite of the fact that Bill faces normal trials, his life has been revolutionized by what the Lord is doing in this outpouring of the Holy Spirit.

THE TESTIMONIES SPEAK

Luke wrote in Acts that a sense of awe pervaded the atmosphere of the early Church and that many wonders and signs were done in the name of the Lord Jesus Christ. This began happening to us. People, filled with awe, began to testify to the work of God in their lives—many of them exhibiting His power over them by outward signs like shaking. As the sense of awe began to pervade the meetings, wonders and signs kept occurring as though the Holy Spirit loved to display His works of power to delight us.

It was as though we had finally found out what church was supposed to be like, everyone in awe of the dynamic presence of God invading their lives and changing them.

Within weeks of the outbreak, five people were healed of diseases, medical facts confirmed by radiologists' reports. People who had felt that God had abandoned them came out of despondency. As I continued to receive prayer, the panic attacks I had suffered from for nearly eight months gradually subsided and disappeared.

Living in renewal since 1994 has given us a new expectation that when we pray, God is going to hear and answer. This is a far cry from the agony of previous years when we braced ourselves for bad reports and felt hopeless about the outcome no matter how hard we tried to believe.

When you open the door of the church, you hear laughter rather than silence. The Holy Spirit starts moving before the services even begin. People pray for each other and invite the Holy Spirit to come to the service, and it seems to make Him happy.

As we began to connect with God we realized that we want to spend time with Him. It is as though we have discovered a dimension of God's presence that makes us long to be in union with Him, having His mind and heart for our lives. It is a pastor's dream.

Psalm 110:3, which states, "Thy people shall be willing in the day of Thy power," has come to pass before our very eyes. God is fueling the services by a River of renewed passion for Jesus. What was once only spiritual potential is flourishing into reality as more and more people discover that without Him they can do nothing, but covered by His Presence they can do anything He wants them to.

The years pass and we still see the Holy Spirit effect change. God has turned our congregation from a spiritually comatose group of burned-out Christians to a group that is on fire. Although our church has grown, doubling in size, it is still small by some standards. But like many small churches in the blaze of revival it is having international impact.

No one can tell me that this is not God. I have seen too much. I have seen an entire church body exhibit permanent change and become activated because of what some people have called an unnecessary renewal.

As far as we were concerned it was as though Jesus had been knocking on the door of the church of Laodicea: "If anyone hears my voice and opens the door, I will come in and feast with him and he with me" (Revelation 3:20).

For years we had been apathetic, but by God's grace we heard Him and opened the door. And when we opened the door, instead of the rebuke we expected, it led to an intimate feast with Jesus.

Four

Experiencing the Center of Revival

Have you ever considered how often Jesus associates Himself with food? He said He was the manna that came down out of heaven. When He instituted Communion, it was with bread and wine. In practically every scene in which He appears in the Bible, He is preaching about banquets, multiplying food or going to eat with sinners.

The religious people faulted Him for this and accused Him of "being a winebibber and a glutton." Apparently sinners in those days had better parties than religious people and Jesus loved parties. His first recorded miracle was at a party where He turned water into wine. He even promised us that eternity would be a feast, the Marriage Supper of the Lamb.

This is not surprising when you consider that man's first sin involved something to eat. The forbidden fruit was a replacement for God's presence. Jesus' only instruction about fasting went something like this, "If you're going to fast, do so only when the Bridegroom is taken from you and for heaven's sake don't tell anybody about it." He wanted His followers to be feasters, too, and not look like the fasting Pharisees who had no reason to feast.

When the presence of God comes as He does in revival, you can spiritually "taste" Him. "Oh, taste and see that the Lord is good" becomes real when you realize that Jesus broke bread with the discouraged disciples after they had walked with Him on the Emmaus road. The first sign of His presence was that their hearts became "strangely warmed" while He talked with them. Later as they asked Him to stay and eat with them, He broke the bread and as they tasted what He blessed, their eyes were opened to see Him.

He is the manna that comes out of heaven, not of our own doing, but graciously falling while we are asleep. If we continue feasting on Him and never allow ourselves to grow tired of Him, He will keep coming until the day we cross Jordan to live with Him forever.

This is the central place of revival: It is called renewal. I believe that we need to partake of this spiritual food daily. We need His presence or we will starve. A Christian who lacks His daily bread will be an undernourished version of the person God wants Him to be. We are like the Prodigal Son, hungry for his father's love; we will starve unless we return to our Father's table.

When God opened the door to this feast for me, I quickly became addicted to His love. I found myself wanting to lie under the weight of His presence by the hour. Doing for Him is not what He created me for; loving Him is. Feeling His love for me kindled my desire for Him. Some days when I feel distant from His love, I feel dry. Before, I did not notice this. Now I do and I refuse to tolerate it anymore. I know now that He created me with a daily need to be nourished by His love. He promised that even though a mother might forget her child, He would not forget me.

In the beginning it is important to run to the table and let God know that you want to experience His love like this. You are living in a day when God is opening the door to this banquet to anyone who wants Him. Allow others who have been feeding on Him to pray for you by simply asking the Holy Spirit to come.

Many Christians like me seek *revival* but do not realize how badly we need this ongoing *renewal*. How often I have heard people echo the aphorism "We don't need renewal, we need revival"! The Bible, however, talks more about renewal and our need for it than revival. In fact, the word *revival* is not even in the Bible. Both of these words suggest a dimension of the Holy Spirit's presence that we do not commonly know. They lift believers beyond "business as usual" and into the jet stream where we find ourselves co-laboring with a supernatural God.

We are hungering; Jesus is calling us to feast on Him. Let's continue to lay a foundation for understanding this central place of revival so that when it comes we will enter the banquet room with joy, our hungering finally sated with food that lasts.

Now we will explore what it means to be living in the center of revival.

Renewal at the Center

Why do we need renewal? Quite simply we need it because we grow tired of living in a realm where we cannot physically see God. Jesus likened it to being attached to Him as branches are connected to a vine. We need the life-flow that comes from His presence if we are to remain hopeful and produce fruit.

When your inner man is renewed it affects everything about you, including your calling and gifting. In other words, the presence of God will not necessarily turn every believer into a soul-winner, but the life-flow of His presence will make you into a light shining in a dark place.

Then whatever your calling is, the flow of life that comes from His presence will restore it. If you are an evangelist, you will win more people to Jesus than in all your years of trying. If you are a church planter, you will plant churches like never before. If you are a prophet, you will begin to see farther than you have ever seen before. If you are one who shows mercy, showing the compassion of the Lord will be energized by the reality of His love.

After only a few days of absorbing the wonder of His presence I was totally spoiled for trying to serve God any more in my own strength; I needed the strength that God supplies. I have learned that without Him I cannot do anything.

Spending time in God's presence actually had an effect on Bill and me physically. Even though Bill had not initially been conscious of anything happening to him, one of our long-time parishioners, Sue Swamckhamer, noted that after we returned from Toronto the first time, we looked ten years younger. This is because hope deferred makes the heart sick, but the newfound trickle of hope that came from God's presence renewed our strength.

While I am not saying that revival is the fountain of youth, I am saying that replenishing your inner strength has great effect. Two years ago at my yearly physical, my doctor remarked. "Your physical condition is that of a woman ten years younger than you are." This is the power of abiding in the Vine, one fruit of feasting on His presence.

The changes are not just physical—or spiritual for that matter. Within weeks of receiving prayer continually, I noticed another change in my life. It was as though God had uncapped a well of cool spring water that began to trickle out of my spirit and into my arid soul—my mind and my emotions. He was restoring my soul, causing water to spring up from a dry place: my own heart. To me it was a miracle of no small proportions.

Bill and I had prayed for people for quite some time with the simple prayer, "Come, Holy Spirit"; I now realized that He had come and I never wanted Him to go. I found myself saying, "Keep coming, Holy Spirit." Every time I said it, my own heart felt strangely warmed as though the Holy Spirit was affirming in me His desire to keep coming.

As I continued to let the River flow up in me, I realized God was creating a garden, a paradise where we could fellowship together. I was the "garden locked" prophesied in the Song of Solomon. I began to spend all my time thinking about Jesus and wanting nothing more than to bask in His presence. I have found that there are no toxic levels of the Holy Spirit. I once believed that receiving too much without giving away was selfish. Now I realize that God was taking His time in restoring my soul. He is continuing the process today.

My focus became Jesus and nothing but Him. I did not care if I ever spoke to another congregation or wrote another book. I did not care how big our church grew or what circles I fellowshipped in. I knew only that I wanted more of His presence.

Prayer became a pleasure, not a duty. Before this, my prayer life had consisted of analyzing needs and asking God to bless and meet them, but now I had entered His rest. I was experiencing His love and agreeing with whatever He told me He wanted to do. Gone was the effort of previous years in which I felt that I needed to pray harder, as though praying was work. Now I was touching eternity, and it was changing my life.

I remember drawing aside in the empty auditorium of the church, lying on the floor there for hours alone. I hoped by this to let the Holy Spirit know He was welcome; but any works of mine did not seem to matter. He just kept coming, disassociating Himself totally from my religious performance.

Then there were times when I felt dryness for no apparent reason. It was as though He was playing "hide and seek" to see if I would miss the pleasure of His presence and run after Him. During this time I began to reread the works written hundreds of years ago by Christians whose passion for Jesus had also taken over their lives. I understood completely when one of them referred to the periods of dryness as "the game of love."

This was new to me; I did not know how to relate to God like this. Keeping Him in focus was often as difficult as keeping up a chase. And yet there were moments when He let me "catch" Him, and I basked in the only thing I have come to want, Him.

Why Is It Difficult to Accept Renewal?

At first letting my heart have affection for Jesus was difficult. Though I am not completely sure why, I think that it most likely came from the emotional wounds of my past. I have come to believe that our past experiences greatly affect our ability to open up to God's outpouring of revival and the ongoing closeness to Him of renewal.

At that point I had written books about the needs of people who grew up in dysfunctional homes and never received affection. I knew that Christians could be affected by these wounds without even realizing what was happening. They are handicapped emotionally and stunted in their spiritual growth because they find it difficult to receive God's love. Here are some of the reasons why.

We Fear Being Vulnerable

Many people in the Church suffer from the feeling that their love for God is unreciprocated. They believe with their minds that God is love, but they see His love as a rigid doctrine, not an experience. Until I felt His presence in revival and ongoing renewal, that was my problem, too. I understood that there was a block to receiving His love but could not get relief from the burden of it.

Gradually, under the influence of the Holy Spirit's presence, I came to realize how deeply I had been hindered. He wanted all blocks removed so that I could enjoy His love and experience His affection for me.

Think about these questions:

Are you a person who has suffered verbal abuse, sexual violation or physical abuse? Have you been the one who has had to look after others all the time? Do you have to "make things happen" or they will not get done?

Do you feel like "freezing" when things around you get too emotional? Do you place a high value on being rational and not such a high value on emotions? Have you dialed down your emotions because you are afraid to feel the pain of living?

Have you made a promise to yourself that you will be careful before you let yourself love again? Or did you promise yourself that you would never allow anyone to get close enough to hurt you?

If you answered yes to any of these questions, it is no wonder that instead of receiving love you probably feel shut down. Emotionally you are a fortress, and opening a door to receive love, even God's love, will become possible only when you make yourself vulnerable to Him.

But can you make yourself vulnerable when you have developed such a longstanding habit of protecting yourself? Is it possible to learn to open up to the love of God?

I believe that you can. Countless people all over the world today in the Church are finding that soaking in God's love is softening the internal barriers they have subconsciously created and tearing them down.

In order to take the first step toward intimacy with God, you need to decide to stop protecting yourself. You need to commit to seeking God while He may be found, while He is pouring out His love like this. You will need to receive prayer as often as it takes for you to let go of controlling your own emotions and begin to feel comfortable in His presence. Being in the presence of God is not always comfortable in the beginning.

We Wear a Mask of Shame

As we learn to be vulnerable and begin to open to God's presence, it is not unusual to experience feelings of shame. In fact, this may be the predominant emotion that wounded people feel in the presence of God. This is because we know we have sinned, not because God wants us to feel ashamed.

Sometimes we feel as though we have distanced ourselves from Him and when others talk about intimacy with God, we wince with conviction that we are not where we used to be. Like Adam and Eve after they sinned and clothed themselves with fig leaves, we look for ways to cover the shame we are feeling at not having done all that pleases God.

Satan, in a desperate attempt to rob everyone of intimacy with God, causes people who are cleansed by the blood of Jesus to feel ashamed over past sins and failures that are not even in God's sight anymore. God the Father has removed every barrier to intimacy with Him by allowing Jesus to die on the cross. His blood shed there removed our sin, not just covered it. *Removed* in both the Greek and Hebrew means "removed."

Yet how often God's people believe that He is recalling our worst moments whenever He sees us trying to pray or experience His love! More likely this feeling is a mirror image of how we are reacting to someone else. If I fail to forgive someone of his sins against me, I will feel unforgiven myself.

While it may be a good thing to pray about, it is not how God feels about us.

One of the primary reasons for shame is the pain of abuse, especially sexual abuse. To have been either a victim or a perpetrator in sexual misconduct unlocks a Pandora's box of shameful thoughts. But every sin we have ever committed or ever will commit was nailed to the cross and permanently removed by the blood of Jesus.

In fact, the only way we can become holy is by reaching out to God, longing to touch and be touched by Him. It is reasonable to imagine, therefore, that Satan, knowing this, wants to use shame to keep us away from His love. If Jesus allowed a prostitute to kiss His feet and wipe them with the hair of her head, He will not stop our displays of affection for Him no matter what we have done.

People sometimes wear religious masks as covers for shame. These zeal-driven saints overdo prayer, fasting and Bible-reading, turning them into performances to prove their worth to God and others. You have no doubt run into them. Instead of talking to God normally, for instance, they employ spiritual-sounding tones when they pray or preach and hold people at arm's length with a barrage of Scripture. Their thinking goes something like this: "I am spiritual. I don't need anything—especially any gifting or ministry that others might have." Their religious masks generate an air of independence as they isolate themselves from people who might hurt them.

These are people who claim to be in the middle of revival and indeed the River is flowing all around them. They effect a spiritual intensity and often try to clamp down on others involved in revival by pressing everyone to do more in order to deserve God's continuing favor, such as more repenting and more discipline. God uses some of these people, but in their hearts they know they are untouched themselves or that they have long since dried out. Intimacy with God is impossible for them until they recognize what they are doing and take their masks off.

Can you imagine the effect that a leader with this approach would have on the moving of the Holy Spirit around him? He would force people out of the realm of rest and back into a shame-based treadmill of trying to earn God's approval either to receive or to maintain revival. People like this often threaten, "If you don't do such-and-such, the Dove will fly!" One thing I have discovered is that the Holy Spirit is looking for excuses to come, not reasons to go.

If you are wearing a mask, taking it off means being real, being yourself. It is O.K. to let your sense of humor out of its religious box or to show God your bad side. Experiencing God's love for you only becomes possible when you feel free to be yourself around Him, to talk to Him simply, like a little child approaching his Father expecting to receive acceptance and affection.

I want to mention a word or two on the subject of joy and laughter, since it is one of the primary signs in this outpouring and one of the hardest for shame-based people to experience. Their overactive sense of guilt precludes their experiencing deep joy.

Did you know that one of the characteristics of adults who grew up in dysfunctional homes is the idea that life is all business and no fun? They have difficulty having fun. This trait surfaces too often in people who cannot seem to let themselves go to God and enjoy the party He is throwing.

They are prime candidates for the "elder brother" role in the story of the Prodigal Son. All the time, they have been good little boys and girls, but they never experience the Father's joy over them or take advantage of the intimate relationship they could have with Him. As a result, they behave like slaves. Oh, their self-righteous morality keeps them inside their Father's estate, but they serve Him without any joy. They have long since left Him in their hearts. That wall of performance must come down for them to experience God's love.

God wants the harvest of returning prodigals to enter a happy Father's home, not a religious, legalistic house dominated by elder brothers who have no intimacy with the Father. If you have taken this role, realize that today God is putting His arm around you. "Come on, Son," He says, "it's time for you to party with Me, too."

We Make Vows and Resolutions

Along with issues of vulnerability and shame, we also have difficulty experiencing God's love because of inner resolutions or vows. These powerful statements were likely made in the face of deep emotional hurt, repetitive disappointment or grief.

Someone who has been deeply wounded might make this resolve: "I will never allow myself to be hurt again. I will never let anyone close enough to do that to me." After all, what if God's will brings hurt or difficulty in the future? Can He be trusted? We cannot bear the thought of being hurt again.

This was my problem in 1994. I had waited so long to see God move supernaturally that it was difficult to trust Him at first. I was suspicious that if I committed to this emotionally, the Blessing would suddenly be withdrawn and I would be disappointed again. But the evidence was too great and the sense of God's love became too strong to resist. I finally let myself go.

Sometimes vows take a different form. We are afraid to make a commitment to God because we will not be able to live up to it. We have too much faith in our shortcomings. We think, *How could God ever love me? He knows what I'll do when temptation comes along.* Or to put it another way, we fear that one day we will have to face a trial that we cannot endure and we will wind up walking away from God.

This is, quite simply, a lie. It is only by experiencing His love that we change. Otherwise not only do we miss the joy of His presence, but we wind up robbing Jesus of our affection as well.

If this is you, you need to hear what Jesus spoke to Peter in his vision about the Gentiles. Peter was a nice, kosher-keeping Jewish boy who prided himself on obeying at least most of the Law of Moses, especially the food laws.

One day he fell asleep on the rooftop patio of his friend's beach house. He saw in a vision a sheet full of unclean animals. All this was complicated by the fact that dinner was being prepared downstairs. Jesus, who, as we have seen, always loves a feast, said, "Arise, Peter, kill and eat."

Peter, excited to obey Jesus but not wanting to make the same mistake Adam made in the Garden of Eden, found himself saying "No, Lord," two words that never belong in the same sentence.

It happened again and again until Jesus said, "What I have cleansed, do not call common or unclean." In other words, anyone I touch and declare holy is holy, even Gentiles. Even you.

Peter's wall broke down and we Gentiles are in the fold today.

When you discover that you have made a resolution that keeps you from change, repent of it. Telling God that you are sorry for making such a restricting vow opens your heart to be able to receive from Him and from others. You also give others permission to enjoy the blessing you have withheld from their lives. Now it is O.K. for you to be blessed, too. It is curious how judgment can close doors on our own lives. Repenting from resolutions opens our lives and our hearts to receive and give love.

Remember, too, that we can limit the joy of His presence if we hold on to cynicism. If you are going to experience God's love, prepare to be in awe. The Greek word for *worship* means both "to kiss toward" and "to be in awe of."

Childlike awe opens the door for us to receive from God and for our faith and hope to rise. If we continue to fear that the door will open to disappointment, we must take another long hard look at our crucial starting point: In order to experience God's presence, we will ultimately have to risk becoming vulnerable.

Letting the Love in You Flow Out

Are you willing to overcome the difficulties that can block the wonderful provisions of renewal? Are you willing to trust Him to remove all that blocks His love?

God wants you to ask Him to fill you with the Holy Spirit. He loves for you to want Him so much that you overcome barriers to receiving prayer. Ask the Holy Spirit to come and expect that He will. When the Holy Spirit begins to fill you, you will feel a burning love for Jesus. The Holy Spirit is setting your affection on Him to bring Him honor. This burning love will purify the motives behind everything you do for Him. Anything He wants you to do, you will do out of love for Him, not the tyranny of "ought to" or the fear of "don't want to."

If your well has been clogged and has stopped flowing, the Holy Spirit primes the pump by pouring in the sense of God's presence. The flow will come out in worship of Jesus and love for other people. You will find yourself fulfilling the greatest commandments of the Law, to "'Love the Lord your God with all your heart and with all your soul and with all your strength and with all your mind'; and, 'Love your neighbor as yourself'" (Luke 10:27, NIV). And you will do it with seemingly little effort.

If you have had any of the difficulties mentioned above, chances are your well has been stopped up, maybe for many years. In the beginning you may feel awkward or shy about it, but it is important to press through these things to experience the pleasure of God's presence.

Sometimes the flow begins as a little trickle. Encourage the Holy Spirit to keep filling you by responding audibly to what you are beginning to feel. Do not ignore even the slightest whiff of His presence. Acknowledge His love wherever you are when it happens, even if all you do is pause at your desk and ask Him to keep coming.

Do not overanalyze your feelings, just feel them. You are "falling in love" all over again with Jesus, the lover of your soul. Tell Him. Tell Him what it has been like to live without Him. Tell Him how you have been longing for more of His presence. Tell Him what He means to you in your own words. Tell Him how you noticed the little personal things He did for you in answer to your prayers.

Do not simply rely on the words of songs others have written. For too long the Body of Christ has thought that worship amounted to a set of songs that made us feel goose bumps. This is only the beginning. Do not stop the flow out of shyness or fear. Let your heart go out to the one Person in the universe you can fully trust.

You may find yourself with the urge to speak in tongues. I remember the Lord saying this specifically to me one day: "Speak to Me in tongues." Your prayer language is meant to be the intimate love language between you and God. No one else's is like yours. The dry soul rarely speaks in tongues and then usually only for intercessory purposes in emergencies. How long has it been since He has heard your intimate language of love for Him? If you have never released it, it is locked away deep in your spirit. Now as His Spirit is filling yours, let it start to flow freely without shame.

If you only knew how Jesus is affected by your worship! He is not stoic at all and is personally grieved when He has to live without your affection. Your worship is a foretaste for Him of His union with His Bride. When you see Him, you will want to spend eternity just looking at Him. In fact, you must die in order to receive a spiritual body that will enable you to experience His love fully and also to reciprocate it in supernatural power.

Sometimes you will see pictures in your mind's eye as you are worshipping. The Holy Spirit is taking advantage of every one of your senses, touching your mind and your thoughts as He influences you to worship Him more. Respond to these by acknowledging what He is showing you.

ENTERING ANOTHER "ROOM"

Sometimes it will seem as though your worship reaches a peak and the flood of God's presence becomes a continuous flow. Teresa of Avila described this dimension of contemplative prayer as rain from heaven, which, in her words, is different from drawing water out of the well with a bucket. When you begin to sense this flow, you will not want to stop it. If it continues, you will think you are going to die from the sheer pleasure of His presence.

In this moment, it will seem as though your heart is fastened to His and love is freely flowing between you. His is a pure, clean love that you can feel, but it is intimate. Some people will begin to wonder at it because it is all-consuming. Passion is a weak word to describe it, but it is what Paul meant when he fumbled for words in writing to the Ephesians: "to know the love of Christ which surpasses knowledge, that you may be filled up to all the fullness of God" (Ephesians 3:19). At this moment, it is better not to speak, only to enjoy allowing His love to go deeper than ever before. Just soak in the flow of love.

There are undoubtedly many dimensions of His love. Enjoy this one to its fullest and always long for more. Sometimes the Holy Spirit will lift you out of our usual worldly realm to see the delights beyond. You will not be able to know when these moments are coming. They are sheer acts of grace.

One of these phenomenal moments happened to me in 1995, four months after I had begun to soak in God's presence. I want to tell you about it to encourage you to let His love flow through you.

I was teaching at a women's retreat and had gone to bed for the night. I felt that my heart was on fire, even about to burst with love for Jesus. I wanted more than anything to move past a barrier that had been hindering my worship. In my mind's eye I felt as though Jesus was knocking over barriers Himself and opening the way for me to more freedom in worship.

The next day after the morning session was over, I was eating lunch when a woman came to our table and asked to hug me. As I reached out to her, the Holy Spirit fell upon me taking away my bodily strength. My knees buckled and I began to cry out in a sound that was something like a wail. I began to shake involuntarily.

Several women helped me from the cafeteria and back into my room. Scarcely had they put me on the bed when my spirit was suddenly sucked up into the presence of the Lord Jesus Himself.

I can hardly find words to describe it. I was hit with the realization that even though everything I had read in the Bible about Jesus is true, it is less than who He is. To be in the presence of Jesus is to be changed by the overwhelming power of His pure love.

In heaven there will not be any need to have your sins rehearsed before Him; when you see Him you will be transformed immediately into His likeness. I felt as though my thoughts and attitudes were immediately adjusted into alignment with His. I could tell where my emphases had been off-balance. I was being fully known. He is the center of the universe and nothing else is even remotely important. I remember thinking, *It is all Jesus, there is nothing but Jesus. Nothing matters in all the universe but Him.* Scriptures were flashing through my mind at lightning speed.

It is true that God the Father has given all things to the Son. By that I mean that no one will have the choice to kneel at His feet; it will happen involuntarily. To be in the presence of Jesus, His all-consuming love, is to be in the presence of the most powerful force in existence. It is capable of destroying our sins and shortcomings.

The Bible says simply, "God is love," because there is nothing else to say. There are no words to describe His beauty. If I could live to be a thousand, there would be no way to forget Him. In a few moments I was destroyed for any other pursuit; nothing else matters anymore except Jesus. If I had had any thoughts before of quitting the ministry, they died that day.

I remember hoping that this was not a vision but that I had truly died, because the pleasure of being near Him was so great. Nothing He wants from me is too much. Anything I can do for Him is not enough. If I could spend the rest of my life worshipping Him, there would not be enough words to do justice to Him.

I realized that I was unable to take in the love He wanted to give me. I was emotionally incapable in my human frame of reciprocating the power of love that was washing over me in those moments. I believe that if He had continued to reveal Himself to me I would have died, and I would not have cared. No one is as important as He is. No earthly possession is worth anything. There is only one luxury, pleasing Him.

I could sense that all He wanted from me was my love. I could not speak except to say, "Lord, Lord." My lips were trembling involuntarily and I could scarcely get out the words, but His love seemed to radiate more when I said them.

What we know as the presence of the Lord on earth is like the farthest planet to the sun in strength and yet it is enough to change lives. Being in the presence of the Lord Jesus Himself scars your face to this world and brands you forever as belonging to heaven.

That was seven years ago as of this writing. I cannot get Him out of my mind. I will not allow anything to distract me from Him. There are now only two things of value: worshipping Him and drawing other people into His arms.

In that realm I could see the depth of His love for others. I could see how dearly He loved every woman in the room with me that day as though a sword had pierced my chest and left my heart hanging open. I wanted to embrace the women and had no words to describe His love flowing into me for them.

The only reason I am sharing this now is to give you hope that all your labor in the Lord is not in vain. It is not worthy to be compared to the glory prepared for you, the joy of His presence.

I have wondered every day since then if it will happen again. I was not fasting or praying when it happened. I did not know that it was possible for a Christian in this life to see this realm, but I did see Him. I did nothing to gain entry. It was a gift of His grace. He wooed me from a place of passionless "Churchianity" and into His very presence.

Since that day I have had to remain content just soaking in the rays of glory that seep into me from that room where He lives. If He wants me to see Him again, I will. Having seen Him only makes me more aware of my need for the Holy Spirit now.

RECOGNIZING THE THIEF AND ROBBER

About the time you are enjoying His presence, do not be surprised if you come under the seduction of the one that wants to rob Jesus of every ounce of glory. Satan went into the Garden of Eden and seduced Adam and Eve out of Paradise. He wants to seduce the Church out of the joy of experiencing the paradise of Jesus' presence.

Satan's main method is taunting, and he will use any means he can, even other Christians, to distract you and get you to eat the wrong fruit. His taunts are usually condemnatory. He wants to make us more aware of our inadequacies and failures than of the presence of the One who fills all in all.

He seems to use two main accusations. The first is that we are not doing enough, a topic that, as we have seen, trips many Christians. It suggests that Jesus is only interested in what we can accomplish. It totally misses the intent of worship. Sometimes Satan will remind us of deeds left undone to keep us in perpetual guilt.

When Mary sat at Jesus' feet to drink in every blessing of His presence, her sister, Martha, bound by duty to cook dinner for the large group of guests, probably started slamming pots around in the kitchen. *Where is Mary? Doesn't she know she's supposed to chop the cucumbers for the salad? And set the table? Who is going to help me?* All the fun of feasting with Jesus was evaporating into a flurry of activity, and Martha got angrier by the minute.

How many times have I heard Martha's criticism in this move of the Spirit: "People ought to get up off the floor and go do some witnessing for Christ!" They miss the point that soaking in His presence furnishes the fuel for witnessing. I say we are to "soak and tell." Soaking is seeking Him. Experiencing His presence is the fuel of joy that causes our faces to glow like the city set on a hill.

Jesus loved Mary's hunger to be in His presence. He will rebuke anybody who tries to rob Him of the pleasure of your company. "Martha, Martha, you're careful and troubled about so many things," Jesus chided her gently. "Only one thing is necessary. Mary has chosen the better part and it will not be taken away from her."

Did you get that? Jesus wants you soaking in His presence, feasting on His words and enjoying Him. That is the real feast He wants with you. Church life is not supposed to be a full schedule of man-initiated programs, but intimate communion with Jesus and supernatural interaction with the Body of Christ. The icing on the cake is the pleasure of communicating His love to the lost.

If the enemy fails with the first accusation that we are not doing enough "works," he will try a second one: making us feel ugly before the Lord, reminding us of our sins. If he can get us to eat from the Tree of Knowledge of Good and Evil, he can destroy the environment of intimacy with God that the Holy Spirit is creating with this River. If he can make us feel as though we are unworthy to express passion for Jesus, we will hold that passion in and it will plug up our wells.

The enemy likes to send a cloud of suspicion between us and the Lord so we cannot see how much Jesus loves us. He clouds the stage with a fog of our unworthiness.

How does Jesus respond to these accusations of our unworthiness? The same way He did while reclining one day at a feast at a Pharisee's table.

A woman who was a prostitute saw from a distance that even the most basic common courtesies were not being extended to Him, and she was grieved. Maybe she was already aware that Jesus was the Messiah. Undoubtedly she had seen Him ministering and teaching elsewhere, and it had changed her life.

Here was a woman who had been repeatedly sexually abused and knew very little about how to restrain herself. She broke past social mores and taking a costly vial of oil, poured it over Jesus' feet. It was so potent that its fragrance attracted immediate attention. Then she started weeping. As her tears dropped on Jesus' feet, she let down her hair, not thinking how it would look, and used her hair to rub the oil into His feet.

By this time, the Pharisees reclining beside Jesus were very uncomfortable. Jesus could read their condemnatory thoughts: *If this man knew who this woman was, that she is a sinner, he wouldn't permit this.* Jesus was all too familiar with this kind of thinking. He is familiar with it today when He hears Satan telling us that we are filthy, we need to be cleaner or more healed or more repentant before we express our love.

But Jesus said, "Her sins are forgiven because she loved much." What? Do you mean that merely loving and touching Jesus with my love is enough to cleanse my sins? Yes. He is the great High Priest, the one able to transmit holiness to the people as we soak in His presence.

For our church, life at the center of this revival means that we end every meeting with a time of waiting in God's presence. After the message, either we play a CD or the worship team sings softly as the entire congregation receives prayer and soaks in God's presence. Sometimes the Holy Spirit interrupts our worship. And our works of service have been far more in number and more fruitful from these powerful, intimate encounters with God.

Not long ago on a Sunday morning, I asked each member of our church to answer two questions anonymously on a sheet of paper: What is the most important thing that God has done for you during this move of the Spirit? And, What would you want me to tell the people reading *Keep Coming, Holy Spirit*?

All of the people, from adults to little children, said that the most important thing they have received is the experience of Jesus' love. The most important thing they want me to tell you is that you need to keep soaking in His Presence.

KEEPING CLOSE TO THE CENTER OF REVIVAL

Sometimes the daily business of living in this world pulls our attention away from Jesus, but if we constantly long for His love and give ourselves to worship, inviting the Holy Spirit to keep coming, we will experience only brief periods in which His love is not in full flame. Stay soaked in His presence.

I have often likened it to the game my sister and I used to play as children called "I Spy." I would say, "I spy something pink." Danna Kay would then try to guess what I was spying as her eyes scanned the room. I would tell her if she was close to guessing which object it was by saying "You're getting warmer" or "You're getting colder."

Keeping passion for Jesus is like that, too. The Holy Spirit will let us know when we are getting warmer or getting colder. When we are getting warmer, we will sense His fullness. When we are getting colder, we will wince with conviction as we remember the height of joy from which we have fallen. All we need to do is acknowledge it and go back to His arms.

All-consuming preoccupations, like those things that absolutely have to be done, can pull our attention from Him and cause the water in your well to sink back down. We will worship what we behold and we will become like what we worship. We must return to the intimate place as soon as we can or our souls will once again become dry.

If you realize from reading this that, like the church of Ephesus in the book of Revelation, you once were there, if you remember the height of passion for Jesus that you once felt and now do not, then repent. That means go back. Ask the Holy Spirit's forgiveness and His help to prime the pump, because keeping revival means keeping passionate love for Jesus at the core of your life.

No one wakes up one morning and says to himself, "Gee whiz, today I think I'm going to quench the Holy Spirit." More than likely we are seduced away from the core value of the outpouring, the presence of Jesus. We must keep inviting the Holy Spirit to come anywhere and anytime, responding to His "intrusions" into our lives so that we continue to soak in His presence. Expect Him to show up everywhere.

One day early in the outpouring I asked the Lord, "How long will this last?" His presence was becoming more and more precious to me. I just could not stand the thought of my long-held belief that this was a season that could end.

"How long do you need Me?" He replied.

I said, "Keep coming, Holy Spirit. I don't want You ever to go." He is still with me and the waves of His presence are more powerful than they were in the beginning.

My prayer is that you, too, are experiencing this joy as the center of revival.

Five

It's Not Your Mother's Old Revival

I can hardly believe that I almost missed the entire revival because it did not look like what I expected. For years I had tried to imagine what it would look like. Mainly I thought that there would be droves of people getting saved, that I would spend most of my time laboring in the harvest of souls.

Maybe this phase is on the way if we are to take our cue from what other nations are experiencing. But for our luke-warm Western nations, I believe that God wants to touch the Church first. I can hardly imagine what we would have done to a load of new converts considering who we were in 1994. We would have shamed the repentant into condemnation and discipled them into little Pharisees just like us who knew everything about who God is and what He does. In 1994 my paradigm for revival was the one I had planned because I could not imagine what was coming.

How Can We Want What We Cannot Imagine?

Not long ago I watched a home improvement television show in England. A team of interior decorators, using the motorcycle as their inspiration, redecorated a once-boring flat for a young man whose hobby is motorcycling. When they brought the fellow in to see what they had done, he was in awe.

"Is this what you imagined?" they asked him.

"I can't want what I can't imagine," he replied.

"Wooooooo," I said, eyeing the screen.

Revival is like that. We tend to develop our idea of what God will do based on what He has already done. This seems easy because there are certain unmistakable trademarks of the Holy Spirit's work. Throughout Church history whenever revival has broken out, some universal signs seem to occur.

For one, revival seems sudden—as it did at Pentecost—as the wonderful presence of God invades the ordinary. God usually descends on the hungry and humble and steps aside from the prominent, obvious choices man would make.

For another, revival seems to be a hovering sense of God's presence that descends over a local congregation. He seems to sit there waiting to see what the people will do before He begins to act.

When He moves, the news spreads by word-of-mouth by those who are being touched. Business as usual is set aside as the lost are saved and the Church is revived.

And finally, Jesus is always exalted to the highest place in revival and people who are affected by it serve God for the rest of their lives. They always remember the dimension of His presence that captured their hearts.

This is the way I had seen revival in the past and the way I had read about it in books. But there is another very important and very visible dimension to revival. I discovered during this move of the Spirit that recent Church history revisionists "tidied up" the accounts of early revivals: They left out the signs and wonders that have characterized every move of the Spirit since the first century. They hoped, no doubt, to corroborate cessationist theology and endorse the idea that signs and wonders ended with the early apostles.

Human beings tend to persecute what they cannot understand. I, for one, did not understand many of the ways that God was moving in this new outpouring. In fact, I stumbled over this evidence and almost missed the whole thing; even shortly before my first trip to Toronto, I ridiculed what God was doing there.

When I heard the rumor that people were "barking" in Toronto and laughing uproariously, I responded, "Oh, puh-leaze! Not something else scampering across the screen of the Body of Christ." One night a friend and I laughed until we could not laugh any more at the fact that people were laughing in Toronto. As it turned out, the Holy Spirit touched me that night.

In the wee hours of the next morning I had a dream and in the dream I saw Bill and myself entering a restaurant. This is not unusual since all my dreams are about food, but as the dream sequence continued, I saw on my right a healing evangelist and his wife sitting at a table eating. I went over to them and to my surprise, I began to blurt out to them how badly we needed to see revival.

Suddenly their countenances changed to that of two men. One of them interrupted me and said, "Haven't I promised you times of refreshing from the Lord?"

In my dream I felt as though I were down under the power. I could feel the love of Jesus enveloping me. This dream turned out to be prophetic. A few weeks later, this was my experience in Toronto.

Even then, the unusual reactions to the presence of God nearly drove me away until Guy Chevreau and the writings of several revivalists from centuries past explained them to me. As I searched the Bible and Church history, I made some interesting discoveries. If you want personal revival and revival in your church, you will need to adjust your paradigm as I did to allow God to touch people any way He wants to or you will risk quenching the Holy Spirit.

SOMETHING NEW

People who criticize revivals, believe it or not, are usually the ones who embraced the previous revival. It seems as though it is too much of a stretch for them to recognize the new. Their wineskins are dry and brittle and they can no longer move with what God is doing.

The Pharisees prayed daily for the Messiah and they are still praying today. They missed their day of visitation because Jesus did not look like what they wanted. I know people who are praying for revival but are avoiding Toronto, refusing to go to Pensacola, ignoring Argentina and wondering when it will ever come. I always had a fear that this would happen to me.

I remember trying to tell my Baptist friends about the baptism in the Holy Spirit in the early '70s. I was greatly excited about it, but it seemed as though most of them were deaf to hearing what God was doing. I wondered what it was that made them deaf, and whether or not it could it happen to me.

It was only by God's grace that we found the River. For years our key Bible verse had been, "Do not call to mind the former things, or ponder things of the past. Behold, I will do something new, now it will spring forth; will you not be aware of it?" (Isaiah 43:18–19). The answer to Isaiah's question is that many people will not be aware of it.

When the outpouring finally came into our congregation, people who had been there for years and who had even prophesied about the River left after this outpouring started. Some embraced it for a short time, but when it did not seem to fulfill their expectations, they abandoned it before God had a chance to begin the work among them.

CHANGING YOUR PARADIGM

We need to give God permission to do something new if He wants to, even if it is different from what we have always believed revival to be. I do not know who said, "If you always do what you've always done, you'll always have what you've always had," but he was right. What have you always done? What is your definition of revival and where does it come from? When you picture what God has promised, what does it look like? What if your picture is less than or different from what God is going to do?

Some people's definition of revival requires that we see large numbers of souls being saved or numerous healings. We need to stop trying to force revival into our molds and let the flow of the River take us where He wants us to go. I believe that if we keep soaking, absorbing the life-giving waves of God's presence, we will see God do everything we have ever longed for without the slightest mark of human striving.

In order to change your paradigm and flow with the current, you must experience revival's blessings yourself. You cannot think that you do not need what God is pouring out and stay in the River. God thinks you need it, and He wants to touch you, too.

I have seen ministers take the pulpit in revival meetings without ever having submitted to what God is currently pouring out. They seem to think that the revival platform is a stage for their ministries to become known to the world, that they do not have to be touched. Some received prayer once or twice and act as though that is all they need. They keep right on with the old paradigms and the works that have always bolstered them. And they also miss most of the blessing. When these people take the microphone, in spite of what they plan to teach, the message is that "God's outpouring is not really necessary for me. I am above it."

William Seymour, in the Azusa Street revival that began the Pentecostal outpouring in the last century, used to hide his head behind the pulpit and bow low when someone like this tried to take over the meeting. The Holy Spirit would squelch the speaker as Seymour prayed. I have seen the Holy Spirit bring laughter down on some who were trying to do this, but I have seen others go right on and keep many from the essence of what God is doing.

HUMILITY: A KEY TO SEEING

If only we could all find the place of humility and stay there! It is the key to receiving anything from God and the key to God's making His abiding place with you and me. Humility is something that we no longer have as soon as we think we have mastered it. Humility means that we accurately perceive our places in the Kingdom of God and find contentment there. Humility helps us to see that God blesses us because we need Him so badly, not because we are spiritual enough to deserve it.

Fortunately, the Bible says that we can humble ourselves. The Holy Spirit is the epitome of humility and will help us. We can take the lower seats. I believe that humility opens our eyes to see Jesus as everything and the other brethren as better than ourselves. If we have any victory in ministry, it is because He gave it to us to serve the brethren and bring in the lost, and He wants to bless us because we are precious to Him. He is cooking dinner; we are just helping Him set the table.

Skepticism and cynicism were deeply imbedded in my heart when revival broke out. They are Greek philosophies, by the way, that take root in the heart that becomes hard and proud. Entering into what God is currently doing means humbling ourselves to receive, and often we need to receive at fountains we might usually scorn. I recall, for instance, being agitated that God had moved at a Vineyard church in Toronto. It took a lot for me to go there.

Thankfully, I changed! It was with a different attitude that Bill and I made the twenty-hour drive to Pensacola to visit the services there. It was a long trip, but we wanted to see all God is doing—a different attitude indeed.

When we arrived we were seated in a section with a number of other pastors. I tried to make conversation with the fellow sitting next to me who had come from Detroit. I told him how we had been so blessed in Toronto and wanted to come to Pensacola to experience what God was doing here.

He sneered, "Toronto isn't God. This is God." He was not, of course, speaking for the staff in Pensacola. Perhaps he did not know that most of them had been touched in Toronto a few months before the Father's Day Outpouring started. Remembering my own former narrow vision, I wondered nonetheless how he could so easily dismiss God's work in Toronto and be so partisan and divisive about it.

In any event, attitudes like this keep us far away from Jesus.

Humility, on the other hand, softens our hearts and opens our eyes to our own needs. It is the door to receiving. It always scares me a little to read that the Pharisees sat in the front row of Jesus' meetings and saw nothing. We need to keep the place of humility or we will grow proud.

God gave me the grace to humble myself enough to receive in Toronto and Pensacola, as well as in our own church. And I want to be someone who always recognizes when God visits the Church and receives what He wants to pour out. Sometimes I think that the Lord sends something new to level the playing field. He puts all of us—pastors and congregations alike—in awe and sends us running to the Bible for answers. He wants a chance to touch everyone.

Permitting Him to Touch You

When God started moving in our church, it was as though the Holy Spirit changed from a doctrine into a living Being and started to revive everyone He was around. I began to break down and do something pastors are taught not to do: let people in the congregation pray for me. As I received prayer, I started to feel the increase of deep joy and outward physical signs began to increase in strength.

Sometimes I would laugh until I could not laugh any more. Sometimes I would shake. Sometimes I would jerk as though an unseen force were squeezing my stomach muscles. Each time I experienced some external manifestation, it always gave way to the love of God. The sense of God's loving presence helped me let go of control, and I began to relax when I understood that the Lord had come to stay as long as we wanted Him.

Reviving me was no small task, or so I thought. The first few times someone prayed for me, I fell under the power of an unseen love. I began to realize that I had labored in the Lord's service for years, but more like a slave than a son. I worked hard but enjoyed little benefit of His endearing presence. Now under the weight of His glory, my passion was returning for the God I thought had abandoned me.

I found myself receiving prayer at every service. "Come, Holy Spirit!" I would say, wondering if He would come back. He did.

In fact, before long the Holy Spirit began to come when I had not asked for Him. At first I might be working at the computer when the weight of His presence would come to me. I had to stop and respond even if only to acknowledge that He was there. Sometimes I could only say how glad I was that He had come and that I never wanted Him to leave, and remain there immobilized wanting more of Jesus' love.

Then the Holy Spirit started coming when I was out doing daily chores. One day Bill and I pulled up in the parking lot of a large store. The back of another car in front of us wore the bumper sticker that says, "Life's too short to drink bad wine!" I burst out laughing knowing that the Lord had directed our footsteps and caused us to pull up behind that car. Now full of the Holy Spirit's new wine, I found it hard to stop laughing. I laughed in the store so loudly that Bill could hear me at the other end of it. I was still laughing when we checked out.

Each time something like that happens, I sense an increase of God's presence and an overwhelming hunger for Him hours later.

I remember looking at the Bible one day and noticing a change in my attitude. I was hungry to read it. It had always been hard for me to read the Bible. Honestly, I only read it to get a message ready for a meeting. Now I could not get enough of reading about revival and studying about Jesus. I enjoyed watching my paradigm change, letting God blow apart my set notion of how He should act. I realized that like the Pharisees I could box Him into my interpretation of Scripture and miss Him entirely.

I believe that the Bible is the infallible Word of God and is the basis for our belief. It proves that we are to have supernatural faith and practice, including encounters with God. Thus, it follows that others who hold the Bible as authority want to know whether or not everything happening today is biblical.

Bill responds with the distinction between *unbiblical* and *non-biblical*. To be unbiblical means that the doctrine or practice is not supported by sound doctrine and should be rejected. To be non-biblical simply means that for whatever reason, it is not in the Bible and will not affect our faith. For instance, offering plates, air conditioning, organ music, flowers on the altar and Sunday bulletins are all non-biblical. We accept them, but they are not in the Bible.

How does this relate to the phenomena we are experiencing in this revival? If you examine them, you will find that practically all of them are biblical. Some are non-biblical. I do not believe that any is unbiblical.

LAUGHING IN THE SPIRIT

Let's start with the laughter everyone is talking about. While everyone usually believes that weeping is the predominant manifestation in revival, remember that this is not your mother's old revival. Why do we believe that God is somber and that when we want to worship Him we must put on a somber face? If someone tells a joke in church, we laugh, but with restraint. Yet God gave us all of our emotions, and we are created in His image.

Here is a good place to start in our understanding: The Bible says that the Lord laughs at His enemies. How appropriate that when the Holy Spirit starts moving He sends a sign like laughter! Maybe He is letting us know that His enemies are about to be "wasted." It is the laugh of victory. "When the LORD turned again the captivity of Zion, we were like them that dream. Then was our mouth filled with laughter" (Psalm 126:1–2, KJV).

Another reason for laughter is pure, unadulterated joy that becomes so intense you have to release it. The idea that God would not have a sense of humor or want His children to be happy enough to laugh is ridiculous. Why would God create us with this ability if He did not want us to use it for His glory? How do you like it when your children are crying and pouting at the dinner table? Is it not far better when everyone is laughing at something mutually funny?

It strikes me that God is throwing a party to celebrate what He is doing. He wants to be with us at a happy time and is thrilled that we are eager to be with Him. It is no wonder that the revelation of the Father-heart of God in this outpouring is accompanied by joy and laughter in His children. If you feel joy and laughter start to well up within you, go ahead and laugh. If your face does not break, keep laughing.

And there is no need to discount the physical benefits of laughing. Laughter releases endorphins into the immune system and promotes an overall sense of well-being. Sadness and depression take a toll on the physical body.

Is that getting into the flesh, some may ask? Well, we need not be afraid of getting into the flesh. We live almost all our lives there. We are rarely afraid of getting into the flesh when we are gossiping, now are we! It only becomes a problem when we might show too much exuberance about the Lord Jesus.

The Bible says that in His presence is fullness of joy and at His right hand are pleasures forevermore. Jesus is the eternal pleasure at His Father's right hand. And guess what? You will be one of the sheep at His right hand if you know Jesus. You are already seated with Him in heavenly places, so I believe your earthly emotional condition should reflect that. If it does not, something is wrong either spiritually, emotionally or physically and you need to find out what.

Maybe your religious tradition or your concept of Jesus makes you afraid to laugh in His presence. Where did your concept come from? Hollywood? Or maybe your mother's admonition: "Don't laugh; you're in church"? Maybe you feel guilty having fun: God is a stern Master and you are a slave. No, you are not a slave; you are a son.

I have heard some people say that they want laughter but have not been able to break through. The laughter of the Holy Spirit bubbles up from within usually for no apparent reason. However, I have seen people laugh at others who are laughing and suddenly find that the well is bubbling up inside them, too. Some of you may recall the first time you spoke in tongues. At first it seemed as though you were doing it yourself, but as you kept on the Holy Spirit began to fill you with incomparable joy and love, and the tongue flowed.

The things the Holy Spirit does always leave a residue of love for Jesus, as they did with me the night my friend and I laughed about the Toronto Blessing. I think that God started laughing through both of us because He knew what He was about to do. I have never laughed so hard in all my life.

One night as the service was progressing at our church and my husband was teaching, I broke out in laughter. I laughed so hard that I fell off my seat and onto the floor. You can imagine that the people in the church were staring at me as if I were some kind of nut. I just kept laughing and then all of a sudden, a little poem came to mind:

"I'm the Happy Farmer, and I'm plowing up the ground,

"I'm plowing up the ground so the seeds won't roll around."

Once I collected myself I wondered if He was telling me that He is using laughter to plow up the fallow ground in our hearts to get us ready to receive something He wants to sow into us. Maybe it is a new revelation of who He really is—One we will love so much that we will tell everybody about Him.

Last year on an outreach trip to a prison in Virginia, we were eating at a restaurant decorated in country memorabilia. We were shocked to look at the wall in the back and see an antique sign proclaiming *Happy Farmer Seeds and Fertilizer.* We knew that the Lord was showing us that He had directed us to be there to plow up the ground and sow the seeds of the Father's love.

If you are realizing that your joy is depleted, ask the Holy Spirit's forgiveness for quenching Him. Ask Him to restore the joy and laughter to your soul.

DRUNKENNESS

Many people have testified in this outpouring to another unusual experience: the presence of God falling on them to such a degree that it feels like a state of drunkenness. Having grown up Baptist and never having had a drink, I find this amusing. But I have experienced it. Laughter has given way to what can only be described as a state of inebriation.

At Pentecost, the mockers accused those under the influence of the Holy Spirit as being "drunk with wine" and Paul tells us that we are not to be drunk with wine but "be filled with the Holy Spirit." He meant to be filled continuously. In other words God wants us to be drunk on the joy of the Lord all the time.

God is rejoicing over the ingathering and wants us to party with Him. It is a sign of God's love and blessing and it is holy. As with the feasts of Israel, no one is to show up fasting and in mourning. It is time to rejoice. Biblical references to rejoicing and feasting far outweigh references to fasts. In fact there is only one day of fasting in the Jewish calendar. I believe that the drunkenness is a sign of the continual feast that the Lord is offering His children.

FALLING

Another revival manifestation that causes controversy is falling in the presence of God. For many years we referred to this phenomenon as "being down under the power." This left many people confused. Unless they feel an external force operating against their bodies, they assume that God does not want them to have this experience.

Overeager evangelists complicate the problem when they lay hands on people for prayer and use force. They give a little push and the person, caught off guard, falls back. This only increases skepticism in all but the most gullible. The honest Christian wants God's presence, not something phony. My husband always says, "It's not about falling; it's about falling in love with Jesus."

Many are hardened by these false exhibitions into assuming that God does not do them or that they have no value. I used to think this way. I would cite the fact that when Jesus rose from prayer in the Garden of Gethsemane, the men who came to arrest Him fell under the power, got up and arrested Him anyway. So if anyone tried to fall in our church, we propped him back up.

The second time I received prayer in Toronto I remember standing there bracing myself because I did not want anyone pushing me. I mentioned earlier that Ron Dick, a prayer team member, came up to us that night and asked if we would like prayer. There was more to the story. Though I smiled and replied that we would like to have prayer, inside I was thinking, *Well, take your best shot. I'll never go down.*

Ron reached out two fingers and gently touched my forehead. Something happened. I began to feel force applied to my upper body. Ron was no longer touching me. I knew that in that moment I had a choice. I could yield or not. I believe if I had not yielded, I would have grieved the Holy Spirit and would have walked away without anything else.

As I lay on the floor, I felt the sense of God's presence and the joy of Jesus laughing over me—a laugh of victory as though He had finally been able to get me to yield to Him. Not falling was a control issue with me. I had made an inner vow that I would not fall, and it was symptomatic of the hardness of my heart.

The idea of falling in the Spirit is difficult for many people. If this has been a stumbling block for you, consider humbling yourself and allowing God to touch you. In order to experience something you may have previously despised, it is a good idea to ask God to forgive you for judging others who have influenced you. Perhaps someone who claimed to have powerful experiences with God pushed you down or failed to meet your expectations. This can block the work of the Holy Spirit in your life.

If you are worried about falling, don't be. It is no big deal. Just lie down. It is so much easier to rest in God's presence than stand as He ministers to you, especially for a long time.

If you fall, stay down. Do not pop back up. If God puts you down you need to reflect on it. Why did He do it? What does He want to show you? Sometimes as people lie on the floor they see visions on the screens of their minds that portray intimate images of the Father embracing them. The Holy Spirit will send wave after wave of His love to wash over you if you respond by lying there lingering in His presence in awe of His glorious love.

There are probably many reasons why God is moving in this manner now. It may be symbolic of the rest He is bringing to the Body of Christ where we cease from our striving and enter into co-labor with Him in the joy of His presence.

Be careful also not to get caught up in the silly quibble over whether people should fall forward or backward. I have seen people searching the Scriptures fervently to validate outward manifestations like falling in one direction or another. The Bible often says that people fell—Saul of Tarsus on the road to Damascus, Ezekiel, John on the Isle of Patmos who "fell as one dead." Well, then, which direction do people fall in the Holy Spirit "as one dead"? I do not know. I guess it depends on from which direction they were shot!

WEEPING

The first manifestation I had after receiving prayer in Toronto was weeping. I wept for relief and joy when the sense of God's presence came trickling back into my soul. I wept for all the years I had missed His presence and because I did not know what else to do to find it. If God had not met me,

I could not have gone on. It was a baby's cry of desperation and my heavenly Father heard me.

Like laughter, weeping gives emotional release. In fact, sometimes people laugh and weep at the same moment, and the sound that comes from them is like a wail. Personally I do not like weeping in front of people; it is embarrassing to me. I normally want to shove down the urge to weep. I had to give myself permission to weep so that God could touch me that way if He needed to.

Sometimes evangelists try to make people cry in the same way others try to make people fall. You can always tell when it is time to turn on the tears, often when "the train is pulling into the station" at the end of the sermon. It is a mild form of manipulation to get people to do the right thing, but it still bugs me.

Genuine tears, however, are a precious sign to God that you deeply care about Him and that your heart is soft. I remember my father watching television during the Vietnam War, weeping as he saw wounded soldiers being carried from the fray and placed on helicopters. He was softhearted enough to respond to the agony of people he did not even know.

God, as the Happy Farmer, often plows up the ground of our hearts by touching us deeply emotionally. He wants our hearts to become soft and warm so that we can both receive and give away His love. Not to allow Him this privilege will quench the Holy Spirit and stop the process of personal revival. Part of keeping the Blessing is giving Him permission to do this and giving yourself permission to cry.

Another reason people cry in revival is because they are sorry for their sins. People who are genuinely repentant sometimes experience a period of sorrow followed by deep joy. The imitation is remorse, which does not necessarily cause a person to make the 180-degree turn back to the Father.

"See to it . . . that there be no immoral or godless person like Esau, who sold his own birthright for a single meal. For you know that even afterwards, when he desired to inherit the blessing, he was rejected, for he found no place of repentance, though he sought for it with tears" (Hebrews 12:15–17). Esau could not find his way back even with weeping. Since Jesus opened the way for us through the cross, let us not just weep, but let us make our way back now while we still have time.

Never quench the Holy Spirit. Seize the moment He moves upon you. If you feel the well begin to open, choose not to choke back the emotional response. It is an outward sign that God is moving within and that you are ready to respond to His overtures of love. Let the River flow.

Strange Noises

Are people really barking in this revival? No. I have been to approximately 270 services in Toronto. I have received prayer more than 2,000 times myself and spent more than 4,500 hours in renewal meetings in Toronto and other places since 1994. I have never heard barking as though people were imitating dogs. Considering the powerful blessings we have received over the years, though, Bill muses that "if they were, they'd be barking up the right tree!"

I have heard "groanings too deep for words" (Romans 8:26). And I have seen people so powerfully affected that their diaphragms are squeezed by the power of God; the sound that comes out of their mouths is like a "yip."

This was a common manifestation during the second Great Awakening in the Cane Ridge, Kentucky, meetings in 1801. Those meetings resulted in more than 25,000 conversions, which speaks volumes about whether or not the Holy Spirit was moving upon the crowd.

OTHER PHYSICAL MANIFESTATIONS

When God's presence and power invade a human soul, it is with great restraint. He probably wants to touch us more powerfully than He does, but He does not want to frighten us. If we were to see Him as He is, we would die—or want to—before our time on earth is finished. But sometimes in revival God's presence comes down as though He almost cannot wait. He came down on Mt. Sinai with fire and it frightened everyone. The writer of Hebrews says that we have not come to a mountain that cannot be touched. Instead, the mountain, the presence of God, is coming to us.

Because of Jesus' blood the barrier of sin is removed. God wants to be close to you, and sometimes He wants to let you know that He is more real than you have been aware that He is. When the Holy Spirit comes upon a person, He fills the human spirit; He touches the soul and sometimes it affects the body.

I mentioned above one sign that happened during the Cane Ridge Revival. Another was that people's heads began to snap back and forth. One account described a woman whose neatly pinned hair came down and began to snap so violently that it cracked like a buggy whip.

In this current revival some say that they felt the presence of God so powerfully that their diaphragms contracted in a manner similar to a woman in birth pangs. I have seen grown men and women in the throes of this experience who later testified that a new season began in their lives or a new ministry came to birth.

One night as I was testifying in front of an audience in England, Carol Arnott crept up behind me and began to pray for me. I did not know anyone was behind me, but I felt my knees buckle and they looked as though they were about to give way.

At other times I have felt glued to the floor as though the *kabod,* the glory or the weight of God's presence, was resting upon me to immobilize me. It took too much effort to stand up. On still other occasions, the presence of God caused me to tremble as though my insides were coming apart.

I have seen others transfixed in a standing position. As we prayed for people in Nagaland, a remote province of India, we saw the Holy Spirit grip little children around the age of eight years old. They would stand for over an hour in one place with tears streaming down their faces as they felt the love of God.

I never experienced any of these things prior to the beginning of the outpouring in 1994. In each case, when the manifestation subsides, I seem to settle into a renewed ability to drink in the love of Jesus as though an earthquake has opened my heart for more of Him.

Gold, Oil and Rain

This outpouring of the Holy Spirit has brought a number of other signs that I personally had never seen before. Some of the most unusual and most commonly reported are gold dust and gold teeth.

At a conference in Toronto in 1999, John Arnott played a videotape of a woman at a meeting in South Africa who received gold teeth; no dentist had put them in her mouth.

During that conference the same phenomena occurred several times. I remember seeing one Asian woman with no fewer than nine gold teeth in her mouth. The gold fillings, placed in her mouth supernaturally, were juxtaposed next to ones placed by the dentist. The difference was obvious. The gold placed there by God was so brilliant that when the light struck it, it caused you to exclaim.

Recently a woman dental technician from Germany testified about the gold teeth the Lord created supernaturally in her mouth. When she opened her mouth, the gold teeth glistened in the light shining on the platform. People actually gasped in wonder.

Our associate pastor, Bev Watt, came home from Toronto with a shiny gold tooth. She requested her dental records and found that the dentist had repaired the tooth in question with a porcelain crown.

Gold dust has fallen in a number of meetings worldwide. There have been occasions when people thought they were seeing gold dust on their hands, but it turned out to be tiny drops of moisture. This glints in the light like glitter. But there are cases in which it actually happens.

One night we were speaking in a church in England. A worship leader from a church nearby was standing in the congregation with his arms raised in worship. He had recently been through a time of discouragement.

When he lowered his arm, his hand was covered with a gold sheen as though he had dipped it into another realm. The gold covered his entire hand and had a transparent quality. The gold sheen remained on his hand throughout the rest of the meeting and the time of ministry afterward. I touched it myself, and some of the gold rubbed off on my finger and then reappeared on his hand. He later said that it was gone the next morning when he woke up.

On other occasions people have experienced oil appearing on the palms of their hands. One day as I prayed for a woman at a pastors' meeting in Toronto, I was amazed to see pools of oil form in the palms of her hands and drip from her forehead. Apparently there is a natural condition that has the same effect, but this woman does not have that condition. At the time the oil appeared, she was down under the power and seeing a vision of God moving in her city.

I remember hearing Pastor A. J. Rowden of Kansas City, Missouri, an elderly apostle from the Latter Rain Revival, talk about meetings in which the crowds could see rain and feel rain, but they never got wet. During this current outpouring, I have been touched several times with a few drops of water while I was down under the power.

HEALING

Volumes could be written about the mercy God shows us by healing His people. Whenever the Holy Spirit moves, He wants to heal the sick and deliver those who are oppressed of the devil. Many times the healing is linked to forgiveness as the ailing person releases someone who has offended him or who has even caused the pain he is experiencing.

In our own congregation we have seen deaf ears opened, surgeries cancelled and emotional and physical illnesses healed. All who are suffering have not been healed, but there has been such an increase that we can only say that it is a signal of the Holy Spirit's work.

In the Toronto meetings, hundreds of people have reported healing of everything from minor ailments to life-threatening diseases.

One man from Ireland came to Toronto in 2000 with a group from his church to experience the Blessing. Although he was only middle-aged, he had suffered for several years from the ill effects of a series of strokes. He was unable to walk without a cane and his bedroom had been moved to the downstairs floor of his home because he could no longer climb the stairs. His wife is a registered nurse.

As he sat in the congregation in Toronto, he began to experience new freedom of movement in his arm. As the speaker invited anyone being touched to come to the platform, he moved out into the aisle and began walking to the front. Then he noticed that he was walking without a cane. Within minutes, his body was fully restored from the effects of the debilitating strokes. When he got off the plane in Ireland, his wife was incredulous. Not only had he experienced the Father's love, but His healing mercy.

NOTHING

Then there are those who have no outward manifestations and who initially feel nothing. But as they keep receiving prayer their hunger increases, and then it is as though the Holy Spirit seeps into their souls until their love for Him is restored to fullness.

I have seen people touched powerfully outwardly only to walk away from the Blessing, and I have seen others who did not seem to have any outward manifestation stand as faithful sentinels guarding the presence of God in their midst because they love Him deeply.

DISCERNMENT

Some leaders want to know how to discern whether or not every sign is from God. The answer is that you may not know when it first happens. God will very likely invade your comfort zone and you must allow Him to or you will quench the Holy Spirit. God is testing you to see if you are willing to risk making a mistake or letting things get out of your control because you are hungry for Him.

What about discerning fruit? You never see fruit the first day seeds are planted. Sometimes it takes a while to tell if the outward manifestation is really a signal of a deep inner work of the Spirit or if it is simply the work of a person trying too hard. Even in these cases, usually no harm is done.

Demon possession is another instance that warrants discernment. In these past years of renewal I have seen a couple of demon-possessed people try to disturb meetings. Usually the signature signs are religiosity, a "God told me" attitude along with rebellion against authority. If they do not respond to a quick prayer for deliverance, employ other measures. I like what one preacher said: "Cast them and the demon out."

Any true sign or wonder is a token of grace pointing to Jesus. This is the case in all the churches where the Blessing is falling. We should not despise signs, but neither should we place more emphasis on them than we do intimacy with Jesus. The best thing is just to let them happen without quenching them. Signs and wonders will follow the preaching of the Gospel and cause people to perk up and pay attention to the Lord Jesus Christ.

May we receive them as blessings and treasure them as moments of His power that we remember always. Tell your children and grandchildren about them so that they can know that Jesus is real and able to do so much more than we have ever expected.

Six

Why Revivals Wane

One Sunday morning in 1978 Mary and Elliott Tepper, who later founded Betel, an international ministry to drug addicts, visited our church. Elliott began to prophesy during the service, and at that time I doubt that any of us knew what he was talking about. He spoke these words: "Prepare to contain the Blessing." We did not know then, of course, that many would refer to the outpouring as "The Father's Blessing."

Elliott went on to encourage us to get ready so that when the Blessing came we would not be like children playing in a sandbox, letting it slip through our fingers like so many grains of sand.

We remembered this word of exhortation. Ten years later in 1988, we even posted a banner across the front of the church saying, "Prepare to Contain the Blessing," but not knowing what the Blessing would be like, we did not know how to prepare. We only knew that we did not want it to slip through our fingers.

After observing the ebb and flow of revival in the Church for at least two and a half decades and watching the longevity of the Father's Blessing, I am convinced that revivals wane only because the people who are touched by them let them wane. They allow the precious Blessing to slip away.

Why people withdraw from God after seasons of blessing is a great but sad mystery. The children of Israel saw God's marvelous feats and expressions of His Father-heart protection repeatedly in the wilderness. But after each miraculous provision they still could not trust Him not to abandon them. That core lie became a self-fulfilling prophecy as they spurned His affection time after time. Finally learning to trust Him took too long, and an entire generation died in the wilderness. They refused the opportunities offered them and missed the Promised Land.

Similarly, revivals wane because we are not ready to appreciate what God is doing. We may welcome Him in the beginning, but we do not really trust Him to stay and keep functioning in that level of power. Nor do we know that holding on to what God does in revival will result in greater blessing. Instead, we tend to make assumptions and allow distractions to cloud our focus and pull our attention away from what God is doing.

In this chapter and the next we will look at a variety of reasons why revivals wane and see how we might be more tenacious and hold on for more.

Deceptions Lead Us Away from Revival

I can declare without hesitation that revival fades because we cling to deceptions about it. Here are the three main deceptions that quench the outpouring of the Holy Spirit in our churches and in our lives. As you will see, they are closely connected as well as prevalent in our thinking.

"REVIVAL IS TEMPORARY"

By far the most common deception about revival is the belief that it is only temporary. In fact, more people in the Church are seduced away from revival by this assumption than any other single factor. Many people are taught to believe this.

If God means for revival to be temporary, however, why then does He send it in every generation? I believe that He is looking for the generation that will treasure the outpouring of His presence and follow wherever He leads.

As John Arnott says, "If you believe that it is over, it will be over for you." People who believe revival is on the wane are destined to see it wane. Their sense of awe is lost. They begin to speak of it in the past tense. A gap develops between what they once experienced with God and what is happening, or rather not happening, with them now.

The companion deception to the transitory nature of revival is the idea that God likes business as usual, our regular program of operation. So after a brief period we get back to it.

These teachings do not align with Scripture. The Bible reveals a supernatural God who works in signs and wonders to draw the lost to Christ. He wants the Church to maintain fervent passion for Jesus, a willingness to lay down her life for her Bridegroom. But on any given Sunday or weekday throughout the world, unless God-initiated revival is welcomed these things are not happening. Religious traditions of every sort replace the active presence of God.

Particularly in the West, church groups are rewarded for institutionalizing themselves, turning into well-greased ecclesiastical machines that function like a business. Our leaders are considered skilled if they have the business acumen to market their churches better than the ones down the road. But many of these leaders and laymen alike wear masks that belie their feelings of powerlessness because they know that Jesus planned for His Church to be more than this.

Sometimes they defend business as usual by saying, "God gave me the vision for our church, so we can't let revival or renewal interfere with it." If renewal begins to supersede the program they believe God has set, they close the door to the Holy Spirit.

"Dryness Is Inevitable"

While it is possible for leaders to stifle revival in their churches, any person can quench revival in his own heart. This is prevalent during "dry spells"—times when God seems far away.

If we believe, first, that revival is temporary, then we are likely to interpret a dry spell as the natural conclusion of God's blessing. Satan, who wants to disturb the intimacy we have with God, bolsters this deception. He will lie to us, telling us that God is going to withdraw anyway so we must make the best of it, salvage what we can and brace ourselves for the worst. If we buy this, we will not expect another wave of His presence and will dry out completely.

Sometimes Satan will spiritualize this deception by suggesting that we must now go back into the desert so that God can "deal" with us. As with most deceptions, there is a small grain of truth in this. God does refine us in wilderness experiences, but His chief purpose is to draw us closer to Him. As this is the heart of revival as well, it does not follow that He wants us to lose the intimacy we have by seeking it in a desert of isolation and despair.

Even in Israel's wilderness lessons God wanted His people to become dependent on Him rather than circumstances. He never wanted them to suffer without Him or to lose a sense of His closeness.

The belief that revival is only temporary defeats a person before he begins. Then when any circumstances seem to verify the loss of God's presence he, like the Israelites, adopts a "See, I knew it" attitude. This is really a deeply entrenched, "bitter root" expectation that he will be abandoned. People who suffer from a fear of abandonment expect it to happen; they do not expect God's presence to return. They do not realize that God wants His children to desire His love so much that we keep resting in Him, regardless of circumstances.

Think about it. Is it conceivable that God would call a worldwide season of blessing to a screeching halt, rob thousands of Christians of intimacy with Him, and send millions to hell just because you and I are in a dry spell? I don't think so.

Nevertheless, when it happens too many people simply let go of the expectation that the Holy Spirit will keep coming. And this lack of expectation quenches His presence in their hearts.

All Christians will probably go through dark nights of the soul when circumstances seem to suggest that God does not love us. All the great men and women of the Bible certainly endured desert experiences; they faced arid places with no help coming from the "landscape" around them. It was a refining fire that caused their character and faith to emerge.

I felt that I was in just such a dark night waiting for my promises from God to be fulfilled. In hindsight, I believe that He wanted me to endure those years by experiencing His love rather than the way I did. But He has used the powerful return of the sense of His presence anyway during this outpouring in my life. It is a priceless treasure to me because I spent years muddling through ministry, trying to figure out where God was. I want to hold onto Him, even if other dry spells come, because I do not want the sense of His love ever to leave me again.

Keeping revival means keeping intimacy with God, maintaining passion for Him alone, trusting Him through any circumstances. He wants us to fix our gaze on Him and follow Him in the same way Elisha fixed His eyes on Elijah, not wanting to lose sight of him until the mantle fell.

"God Is Hard to Please"

"Revival is only temporary." "The circumstances indicate that He has gone from my life." Soon on the heels of these false perceptions is this companion fear: It is easy to lose God's presence because He is hard to please. We believe that He is really like a dysfunctional father, full of rage. We tiptoe around on eggshells fearing that He is just waiting for us to step out of line.

When we enter a dry period in which we cannot feel His presence, we blame ourselves. We fall into the deception that He left because we did something to offend Him. What is wrong here is our view of God, a view that He has come to correct in this outpouring. We lose sight of the fact that He is a loving Father looking for ways to bless rather than reasons to leave.

Personal experiences of abandonment add to this fear. People who were raised to believe that any happiness in their world will evaporate will have trouble trusting that God's blessing is permanent. If my earthly father left me, either by death or by abandonment, my heavenly Father will, too.

Belief in such an isolated, disinterested God is a form of Deism. To these people the Church is like a clock: God will just wind us up in a period of revival, step back and let us tick ourselves down.

For myself, being charismatic and believing that revivals were temporary and fearing that God was hard to please all made me into what I call a "cyclical cessationist." I used to believe that we would be supernaturally invaded once every decade for a period of a year or so, so we needed to brace ourselves for a lifetime of the worst. This was especially frustrating to me because I have never felt successful at "business as usual." I am awed by the fact that we are entering our eighth year of outpouring and that His loving presence only increases.

We must learn that God is utterly reliable. His love is perfect and unchanging. Too often His reliability is filtered through the lenses of our own compulsivity. God is not compulsive like us, driven by external forces in and out of focus on thousands of different things. Americans are some of the most impulsive people on the face of the earth, suddenly getting in, but just as suddenly getting out whenever we become bored with anything. God is steadfast in His purpose and His love. He is not easily turned away. And if we hold on to His presence, we will find ourselves continually in awe of what He wants to do.

DISTRACTIONS QUENCH REVIVAL

We have just examined several deceptions that open us to discouragement, to letting go of the presence of God and to stepping out of revival's mainstream.

Anyone who surrenders to these core lies is also in danger of embracing further distractions that quench the Holy Spirit. Remember, the Bible does teach that it is possible to "put out the Spirit's fire" (1 Thessalonians 5:19, NIV). Here are some obvious and not so obvious behaviors and beliefs that quench the Holy Spirit.

POLITICS

Jonathan Edwards believed that the Great Awakening in Northampton, Massachusetts, waned for several reasons. One key factor was that the townspeople became distracted by political issues. Apparently an election arose over a community matter and people began to take sides. They let go of the awakening after only two years. For the next decade the awakening resurfaced a couple of times, but because they did not know that they were to treasure it, they eventually quenched it.

The tendency for politics to distract the Body of Christ happens often, particularly in America where people are encouraged to have an active political voice. I believe that God has called men and women to serve their countries in government, but when revival comes, politics has at best a backseat.

I heard the late John Garlington say once, "There will be no American flag over any of the twelve gates." Isaiah said, "Surely the nations are like a drop in a bucket" (40:15, NIV). And I do not read in Scripture that the apostle Paul advocated demonstrations against the Romans for their genocide or the carnage in the Coliseum. He was serving the King of a higher Kingdom, which will one day come to earth in all its fullness. When revival comes, God lifts our vision to Him where there is no time and no authority higher than His.

I remember those moments when I was caught up into the presence of Jesus and saw how everything else paled in comparison. I especially saw that my own tendency to look into the political arena for relief for my country was off base. While I pull the voting lever regularly and support the views of one particular party, I am not giving myself to championing political causes while revival is in the earth. His Kingdom is not of this world.

Survivalism

Another distraction closely aligned with politics is survivalism. It seems that in every revival people recover an urgent sense that Jesus could come at any moment. When we read the book of Revelation, particularly with Western linear thinking, we note that the Antichrist comes and spiritual warfare occurs at the end of the age.

Some, however, develop a survivalist "them and us" mentality and begin to cower in fear of calamities that might take place. They sometimes withdraw from God's presence and prepare for battle as though anything but basking in His presence would prepare them for what is ahead.

During times of revival, I have seen the enemy inject survivalism into many people. A number of people, for instance, who stored food and water under their beds and worried about how computers would survive the millennial change, also armed themselves to protect their provisions. When nothing happened, many of them were embarrassed. Long ago they had become distracted from what God is pouring out because they were focusing on this world rather than trusting Jesus.

As Jesus ascended into heaven, the angel of the Lord told the disciples not to stand gazing after Him as if looking for His return. He said that when Jesus comes back we will all know it. We are instead to follow Jesus' instructions in the power of the Holy Spirit. Prophecies that inject fear into the Body of Christ are not from God, no matter who is giving them. They are not edifying, exhorting or comforting and, therefore, not endorsed by New Testament theology.

Now it is true that sometimes God warns of lean years, as when Agabus prophesied to the early Church about a famine to come. However, the Bible points out that this famine did not occur until some time later, during the reign of Claudius. The early Church did not respond in selfish fear but took up an offering for the brethren who would be affected by it, a far cry from the way most of the world responded to Y2K! The intimate knowledge of Jesus' love that comes in revival is the insulator against any storm we will face.

Too Much Looking Ahead

Another distraction seems well-intentioned but it, too, serves to take the focus off the presence of God: This is the preoccupation with intercession and prophecy. Both of these spiritual gifts have increased in places involved in the outpouring, but if we spend all our time wondering what God is going to do next, we will miss the glory of what is happening now.

Richard Riss, professor at Drew University and church historian, has commented that other revivalists in the past made the mistake of thinking that their current move was only the herald of a greater wave. Most of them never lived to see the greater wave. I believe in prophesying, and I believe firmly in a greater wave, but I also believe that I need to be content with what He is pouring out now; what He is doing now is preparing me for what is ahead.

Matters of the Heart

Edwards also believed, as did Charles Finney, the nineteenth-century American revivalist, that matters of the heart could quench the Holy Spirit. This is only true, of course, when individuals grieve Him by choosing in their hearts to commit sins. They ignore both their consciences and the Holy Spirit's conviction.

God sends revival to sinners who are in need of a Savior and to lukewarm church people who need a fresh touch from God in order to turn from sin.

There is a distraction that snags sincere Christians seeking revival, however, and it has an unusual twist: Many fall into the subtle sin of searching their own hearts for sin to excess. This is not unlike the examples we noted earlier regarding those well-meaning Christians who try to generate revival by pious deeds. Those who develop such an inward look run the risk of falling under the hand of the accuser of the brethren. If they cannot find a specific sin, they feel they are not fasting enough or praying enough or reading the Bible enough. The focus shifts to them and their flaws and they lose hope.

Subtly the enemy continues to accuse them, threatening that God will withdraw unless they locate the problems with their hearts—if not sins then emotional areas that need inner healing—and deal with them. Rather than wait patiently for revelation, they try to dig them up.

To believe that the Father is going to subtract His presence because we cannot uncover every sin we have ever committed is more bad news than Good News, especially when we read in Scripture that we cannot know our own hearts.

One day Bill and I were standing in a stadium where a large revival event was about to begin. Tino DiSienna, our pastor friend from New York City, commented in his delightful Bronx accent about the intensity of the preaching he was hearing.

"You know," he said, "when I go to Toronto, I feel that God loves me. But when I come he-ah, I feel that I need to get saved all ova' again. I'm trying to rememba' if I stole a matchbook in the seventh grade."

Few people can stay eager for God's presence when they are distracted by trying to uncover sins in order to be worthy of His presence. While we must always confess known sins and turn from them, we need to remember that it is the kindness of God that motivates us to repent.

We Simply Lose Interest in Revival

One night before an intercessory prayer meeting, I found an article in the February 1998 issue of *Texas Highways Magazine* entitled, "There's Something in the Water." According to the article, throughout the nineteenth and early twentieth centuries it was a fad in Texas to vacation at several towns that boasted mineral springs. Towns like Mineral Wells boomed when people came to believe that the water in their springs had healing properties.

Apparently this was not too far from the truth. One well in Mineral Wells is called "The Crazy Well." A woman in town who seemed to be suffering from incapacitating mental illness began to drink repeatedly from this well and regained her sanity. That kind of news traveled fast and people came from far and wide: presidents, entertainers, foreign visitors and regular folks. They came for two reasons, to drink the water and to soak in it. This sounds like a picture of revival to me!

As time went on, people whose suffering had been relieved, including several medical doctors, held testimony meetings near piles of crutches and medicine bottles left at the wells. The common experiences generated camaraderie among the seekers and soakers.

Soon the wells began to generate a resort atmosphere where the sophisticated came for rest and relaxation. Large hotels were built to house the tourists flocking to the healing waters. Bands played, people shopped and kept drinking and soaking in the water.

Then in the 1950s the advent of television and the invention of antibiotics caused people to lose interest in the wells. Today the wells still flow with the same water that was reported to have healed thousands. Some of these towns still export their water all over the world, but the great fervor has died down.

A few months after I found that article, I met a pastor's wife from Mineral Wells, Texas. I was invited to speak at her church and I preached from Isaiah 42 about opening wells in the desert. I learned later that her husband, the pastor, had been appointed head of the civic committee to restore the wells.

The application to revival is clear. God's well never dries up nor does it lose its healing power. For one reason or another, we just stop going there and withdraw from Him. Like the people who abandoned the mineral wells, it is usually because of some substitution for what we have found at the well. People find something else to put their faith in.

Here are several reasons we lose interest.

Emotional Challenges

Sometimes people substitute the euphoria of exciting meetings for intimate fellowship with God. When something new and interesting comes along that replaces the euphoria, they opt out.

Other people who tend to be compulsive often do not trust themselves. They try to overcompensate for it by pushing themselves beyond God's gentle leading. In serious cases this enters the realm of religious addiction. It drives them out of the River and back into performance-based Christianity. It causes them to become increasingly impatient with others and propels them on the addictive cycle of stress, contemplation, obsession, compulsivity, indulgence and remorse. Religious behavior becomes the drug of choice.

More than once I have been tempted to think that those who frequent the altars with repeated repentance are in the remorse phase of the addictive cycle. They will be back tomorrow and the next day focusing on the same problem.

And a word here to those in treatment. Do not let the high of meetings cause you to stop receiving treatment for your addictions and emotional problems. Do not throw out your medication because you suddenly get filled with the Holy Spirit. Time will tell if you have really been set free.

GRIEF

Sometimes people lose interest in revival because they are overwhelmed by genuine hurts and disappointments. Grief, in particular, can take a toll on intimacy with God. Recovery from this takes time. One of the wonderful fruits I have seen in this move is the comfort of the Holy Spirit on people in our congregation who have lost loved ones.

One person I note in particular is Donna Bernd. Donna found the renewal because she was desperate. Her husband had suffered for years with depression. One day after work, while Donna was preparing dinner, he pulled out a gun and took his life.

It is not hard to imagine the devastation from this event. Donna, who testified at church recently, told how soaking continually in God's presence for the last five years has soothed her grief and made it bearable. She has even known periods of deep joy throughout this time.

EXPECTED RESULTS DO NOT HAPPEN

Sometimes people who do not receive what they want from the revival get disappointed. They not only lose interest in it, they belittle it. This is particularly true when revival does not seem to have the desired effect on a loved one. Anger with God leads to embracing many lies. The resulting cycle of despair causes withdrawal from God. They lose sight of the fact that God has His own way of bringing the answer to our prayers.

Another form of disappointment occurs when a leader realizes that the church is going through a lull or that the revival has not tipped or led to the church growth he hoped for. He decides that God must be finished and stops renewal meetings or having soaking times in the services. Sometimes hidden bitterness can even cause him to become angry with others who still want to keep the fire lit.

I do not know that this renewal was meant to grow larger churches. If it is true that contagious messages are best spread by groups of fewer than 150 people, maybe the Lord wants to saturate every church, large and small, with His presence and cause us to be satisfied with Him. Maybe He is about to invade us with another wave of His presence to make the message He wants us to spread even more contagious.

DIVISIONS

Church splits have ended more than one revival. Disgruntled people lose interest in revival but take great interest in leading others into their negativity. They take the seat of judgment evaluating the experiences of others while refusing to enter in themselves. These people are interested only in their own gossip. Their talk spreads like gangrene among people who have little to do but commiserate.

Sometimes the revival itself generates a church split as the old wineskin changes to accommodate the new wine. If the leaders believe that revival brings only blessing or that the Holy Spirit never brings division, they are not prepared for this one. Whatever happens, I believe it is important to maintain intimacy with God as the focus of the revival and the local congregation's core value. God will send in the hungry.

PHYSICAL TIREDNESS AND BOREDOM

Churches that give away the Blessing regularly face all of these difficulties within their ranks—and more besides. It is hard to believe that Toronto has given away the revival Blessing for eight years now, with renewal meetings six nights a week. I have heard John Arnott pray often, "Oh, Lord Jesus, don't ever let me get tired of seeing You touch people like this!" Maybe that is one reason they have been trusted with the treasure.

People in churches who are close to the power of God sometimes get used to it, though, and interest wanes. Even our small congregation has seen nearly 35,000 people come through the doors in the last seven years to receive the renewal Blessing at our Friday night meeting. Seeing the first several hundred people fall and begin to receive His love was exciting; by the time the number reached 20,000 we had to make certain we kept our amazement over what God is doing. I always remember what it was like for eighteen years when nothing was happening. This keeps me grateful.

Sometimes members of churches confuse their behind-the-scenes work of servicing a revival—working in the office, preparing sermons, making arrangements for guests—with experiencing it themselves. It is as important for them to keep soaking in the Blessing as it is to keep working at their jobs. You need renewal in the renewal.

I have often joked, "I'd rather have our secretary jerking than working." Sometimes while Linda Heron, whom I affectionately call "The Secretary of the Eon," is working at her desk, the presence of God comes upon her. She is one of our faithful intercessors. When the Holy Spirit comes upon her she experiences what some revival literature calls "the jerks." She also laughs and weeps and prays. This lasts for a while. To me seeing people outwardly affected by the power of God is one of the treasured aspects of revival Blessing.

That is why our office is here. We are not an institution. We are here to answer the phone so people can find the watering hole, but we need the water, too, if we are to continue answering the phone.

Charles Finney was convinced that one of the main reasons revivals wane is that people grow physically tired. Physical tiredness and boredom go hand in hand. Sometimes we cannot tell which comes first, the chicken or the egg, the physical tiredness or the boredom or the loss of awe. Regardless, people need to refresh themselves with rest, particularly if protracted meetings are to be sustained.

When people become tired and bored, they lose their sense of awe, one of the essential ingredients of revival. During the wane of the previous move of God, we tried to substitute hype for our loss of awe. Hype is fake awe. That is why I dreaded going to Toronto this first time. I said, "God, please, I can't stand to have my motor revved one more time." Fortunately, I saw the exact opposite—the power of God flowing through unpretentious people.

Our friend Warren Marcus is a media genius who produced video accounts of the Toronto, Pensacola and Smithton (Mo.) revivals. Warren is a Jewish believer who found a new love for Jesus in Toronto. He warned us all, "Don't let yourself get tired of this." Warren, who ached with all of us at the waning of the charismatic renewal, knows what it is like to lose the powerful presence of God and sink into a cavern of skepticism.

When we were visiting in Alaska not long ago, Bill read an article written by a cyclist who nearly died of dehydration while riding past miles of melting glaciers and icy springs. Water was all around him, but he made a near-fatal mistake: He forgot to drink. The euphoria of the ride produced a high that masked his thirst. Ask God to keep you constantly thirsty for more of Jesus' love so you do not dehydrate in the River.

Each local church needs to ask the Lord how many revival meetings to have each week. We have Friday night renewal services and Sunday morning services, which look just like the Friday night services. We also plan special weekends when guest speakers who are soaking in God's new Blessing come to help renew our thirst.

God spoke to us, "Consecrate yourselves for the long haul." We have found this pace just right for the size of our church.

One mistake I have seen occurs when churches try to conduct protracted meetings without enough people to serve them. Unless you have multiple worship teams and the majority of your people are in the River and hungry to be at the meetings, it is better to slow down to a pace you can sustain for years. Otherwise, exhaustion will take over. You will lose sight of intimacy with God and the revival will dissipate. It is far better to add meetings than subtract them.

DISAPPOINTMENT WITH LEADERS

Another reason that people lose interest in revival and withdraw from God is disappointment with revival leaders, whether founded or unfounded. When a revival leader falls, it rocks believers with an earthquake of discouragement, particularly those who trusted and respected him or her. Sometimes people have been so disappointed with leader after leader that they are afraid to place their trust in anyone else.

And, of course, people who become involved in revival believing that the new anointing will make their leaders superhuman and without fault are in for big disappointment. Their expectations dashed, they withdraw. It is interesting to note that the parish in Northampton, Massachusetts, that experienced the Great Awakening later fired Jonathan Edwards—not for anything he did wrong, they just did not like the way he handled things.

Disappointed people get critical as the children of Israel did with Moses in the wilderness. When we criticize, we take the seat of judgment. Cynicism and skepticism increase as we take bite after bite of the forbidden fruit of the Knowledge of Good and Evil. We cannot judge anyone else because we can never see his or her motives; we are responsible only for walking in what we know. Removing the finger of judgment is part of the chosen fast spoken of in Isaiah 58.

One time early in the outpouring, God spoke to our church and told us to fast. But He did not want us to fast from food; He wanted us to fast from criticism. When Bill announced it, one man raised his hand and said, "Can't I just not eat?" He spoke for many when he suggested that starving himself would be easier. Besides, it was an election year. For the next several months we refrained from criticism and people often testified of the sense of unbroken communion with the Father as the glory of the Lord became their rearguard.

FRAMING REVIVAL WITH A BOX

Losing interest can be as much a passive stance as active. Building a doctrinal framework around revival, however, is deliberate and kills it.

As I was reading Jonathan Edwards' writings about the outpouring he experienced, I was impressed with the fact that people began to receive gifts of the Spirit. Jonathan Edwards, however, was a cessationist. Although he approved of revival manifestations like visions, transports, shrieking and fainting, he would not allow the gifts of the Holy Spirit to be practiced. He thought it was spiritual pride for a person to think he was receiving a gift of the Holy Spirit because he believed those things had ceased. He was not open to the Holy Spirit restoring any lost biblical truth to the Church. I wonder where the Church would be today if Jonathan Edwards had opened himself to the restoration of the gifts of the Spirit. He may have kept revival from developing beyond his doctrinal box.

R. A. Torrey, A. B. Simpson and other founders of the Christian and Missionary Alliance movement also flowed in revival in which the chief characteristic was intimacy with

God. But when the Pentecostal outpouring came and began to distribute fire and gifts on the Church, they found it difficult to embrace.

When we build a box around revival and say "This far but no farther," we restrict revival's ability to expand our revelation of God. This closes off those in the box from the next thing God does.

In this current outpouring many are receiving a revelation of the Father's love. And although this is the core of the Gospel, we would not want to say that that is all God is doing. This would shut out anyone receiving a revelation of Jesus as the Bridegroom, for example. When we close the box, we seem to be saying, "We've arrived. There's nothing else to know about God."

Time after time God has challenged my unbelief as I have watched leaders flow in the River. When I saw gold dust appear on the man in England and when gold teeth appeared supernaturally in people's mouths, defying their dental records, it challenged me to the core. I have seen healings that I had difficulty believing before because of my hardness of heart. I have seen the Holy Spirit touch people with a variety of effects and yet produce the same passion for Jesus. All of it has shoved out the walls of my previous box, and I want to resist creating another one.

Sometimes just realizing that God wants to stretch us is enough encouragement to reexamine the Scriptures. God may be shedding light on things that have restricted the Church's ability to communicate the Gospel.

STRANGE DOCTRINES

Throughout Church history many revivals have been derailed because strange doctrines developed from those leading them. The early Pentecostal revival in the twentieth century split over the doctrine of the Trinity. The anti-

Trinitarian Pentecostal "Oneness" movement came out of that revival because of conflict with the mainstream. Some of the early healing revivalists became almost cultic in their practices and drew away from the rest of the Body of Christ.

Even differences in widely held doctrines create a breeding ground for disagreement. Whitfield and Wesley split over the Calvinist-Arminian controversy. Whitfield took the Calvinist view that salvation is a foreordained work of grace which cannot be lost; Wesley took the Arminian position that although salvation is given by grace, it can be lost, calling the believer to a life of holiness.

Sound doctrine is, of course, vital. And to discover it we need the Word of God, but we also need the Holy Spirit. Revival usually restores some lost truth to the Church, because the Holy Spirit sheds light on Scripture. When we try to gain understanding through assumption rather than revelation of the Holy Spirit, we will fall into error. Every major error that surfaces in revival dethrones God from the center of the revival and causes people to magnify the doctrine itself or its expositor.

Derek Morphew, author of *Breakthrough: Discovering the Kingdom*, says that every doctrinal error is an aberration of Jesus' teaching about the Kingdom of God. Morphew says that the Kingdom of God has come, is here now and is to come. When we say that the Kingdom has not yet come or that it is not here now or that it is all here now and nothing is yet to come, we fall into error.

Let us fix our eyes on Jesus and our heavenly Father's love and spread the fire, not a doctrine that has no bearing on the Kingdom that is, was and is to come.

God Is Here to Stay

What do we say then? Is revival temporary? Or does it just go underground waiting for another place and another moment to spring up? Or does it flow to another place in the earth that is ripe for it?

The Holy Spirit has never disappeared since the Father sent Him at Pentecost. Throughout the ages the River has been flowing—sometimes like a small stream, sometimes like a raging River at flood-stage, but revival has never totally ended. By the same token, God has been forced by our beliefs into seasonal times of blessing.

While I am grateful for the seasons, I also believe that the glory is to increase, not decrease. We are to be moving from glory to glory personally and corporately as long as we live.

Recently at a conference in Toronto, Dick Mills, whose prophetic words have blessed the Body of Christ for decades, gave me a personal word. It was Proverbs 4:18: "The path of the righteous is like the light of dawn, that shines brighter and brighter until the full day." He said, "This thing isn't going to peak. It's not going to die out. It's going to go on and on."

Since revival comes to restore us to fervent passion for our Lord, any notion that it is leaving is, I believe, from the evil one. If Satan lied to Adam and Eve to disrupt their intimate relationship with God, how long do you think he will allow this happy revival scene to continue without challenge? The same enemy who told Adam and Eve that God did not have their best interests at heart wants to stop you from further intimate contact with God. God is not withdrawing from the Church; why else are thousands continuing to be touched by this outpouring?

To imply that God is withdrawing is contrary to His promise never to leave us or forsake us. Once God opens a dimension of His love to us, He never takes it away. "The gifts and the calling of God are irrevocable" (Romans 11:29). Apparently Paul did not believe that revival should end either. In fact Scripture exhorts us to walk at the level we have attained and be faithful to the light we have received. No scriptural reference says anything about God withdrawing. It is really we who withdraw, not God.

In this chapter we have talked about a number of errors in thinking that spoil revival. Next, we will look at two major blocks to revival—one spiritual, the Jezebel influence, and one relational, a question of unity.

Seven

Overcoming Blocks to Revival

When Bill and I first arrived in Toronto, we noticed something wonderful about the way the meetings were conducted. There were no stars on the platform, no faces recognizable from the shiny four-color pages of Christian magazines. There was a rare humility about the place. None of the men was even wearing a tie. The first time John Arnott prayed for Bill and me, I think he was wearing a sweat suit and chewing gum! *Finally,* I thought, *a revival for regular people like me.* It was like the Bethlehem stable.

It was very different from a revival Bill and I had known about years before that broke out in a large American city in a traditional denominational setting. Beforehand, the elders had talked to the pastor at least once about his sexual misconduct with women in the church. On account of his winsome personality, however, and because the elders wanted to show mercy, they were reluctant to dismiss him. Not long afterward, when God-sent revival descended, word spread that something new was happening, and crowds began flocking there.

The special presence of the Lord hung over the congregation, drawing lost people to salvation and thousands into the baptism in the Holy Spirit. The revival spawned ministries led by many who are still in the pulpit today, some of them serving faithfully all over the world. It should have lasted forever, but something happened that spoiled it. Just as Satan appeared in the Garden of Eden, another influence began to affect the leader, who had never received the ministry he needed to recover from his sexual addiction.

As the crowds began to increase and invitations flowed in from conferences across the country, the leader fell into pride. He was not ready to withstand the temptations that accompanied the flattery of congregants who identified him as the revivalist or the adoring gazes of women who longed for husbands like him. Another snare lay in the area of finances. After years of struggling with an average income, now this leader was receiving more money than he ever had in his life as funds poured into the church from people enjoying the revival.

The temptation proved too much. Behind the scenes, word began to spread of women who had been molested in his office, and the cover-up began. Many people never knew what was happening. Others did and were afraid to confront the situation for fear of losing their own reputations. Who would believe them when the leader was nationally prominent?

The people surrounding the leader were confused to observe the anointing of the Holy Spirit evident in the services on Sunday morning and the leader's flirtatious behavior in the office the rest of the week. It must be that God did not mind his behavior, they decided, and they chalked up what they did not understand to the fact that God is gracious.

The revival was so solidly established, they thought, it could not erode.

But gradually the manifest presence of God that had characterized every service began to dissipate, replaced by hype and professionalism. The leader was compelled to maintain by natural means what had initially been brought about by the Holy Spirit. Members of the staff who feared losing their jobs and who wanted to see the work flourish encouraged him to put his image on every tape or flier that went out from the main office. One of several prominent young men attending this church, who aspired to ministry but who knew what was going on behind the scenes, claimed that the falling leader was his mentor, that he was learning all he knew from him and that he did not want to expose him, as he cited Scriptures on spiritual authority.

A man-centered ministry was now replacing what had begun as a spontaneous, God-initiated revival. The leader was seduced into taking the credit; and decisions by pastor and staff were based on holding on to what they had, rather than allowing God to determine the course.

Within three years of the breakout of revival, all that was left was a megachurch that drew crowds because of the leader's dynamic personality. Within six years he fell ill and died. The young man he had mentored started another church across the city, drawing most of the congregation to his side. But today his church is gone, too, and his marriage has ended in divorce. And thousands of disillusioned Christians wonder what happened to the revival that began in such power that they will never forget it.

What happened? Several factors converged to sabotage what God was doing, all of them satanic in origin, flourishing under cover of darkness, as sin usually does. The leader, and later on his protégé, had more than one weakness that neither of them was willing to face. Pride and the feeling that they were well-insulated by popularity, money and authority made them feel they could never fall.

When situations like this are allowed to continue without repentance, that insidious satanic influence seeks out the people close to power and authority. It attaches itself to situations in which people are insecure and working with impure motives. Its agenda: to ruin what God is doing and destroy lives, often through greed and sexual perversion. Revelation 2:20 calls it "the woman Jezebel," alluding to the evil spirit that must have controlled the queen of Israel who led the nation into idolatry. It can enter even a setting of revival and seduce unsuspecting sheep, male or female, away from the presence of God to do things they would otherwise never have done.

THE JEZEBEL SPIRIT

I almost hate to mention Jezebel because I have seen people use the term to falsely accuse people they disagree with. Situations like the one that occurred in the church I described are fortunately not that common. But if we are to stay in the heart of this work of God, we must allow the Holy Spirit to examine us, remove any hook that the Jezebel-like influence might have in us and flood us with His light.

Here are some of its manifestations.

SPIRITUAL PRIDE

Spiritual pride is the sin that took out Lucifer and plunged him into hell. When you are proud, your spiritual slip is showing, and everyone sees it but you. It is not pride to know that God has given you something wonderful; it is pride to think that you have *deserved* something wonderful. Recall Joseph in his youth. He had received exciting visions from God about how he would ultimately save his family. The problem came when he exalted himself over them, suggesting that he had been given this position because he was God's favorite.

Jonathan Edwards gave this warning in his essay "Distinguishing Marks of a Work of the Spirit of God": "Let us therefore maintain the strictest watch against spiritual pride, or being lifted up with extraordinary experiences and comforts and the high favors of heaven that any of us may have received. . . . When we have great discoveries of God, we should not shine bright in our own eyes."

Edwards went on to characterize pride as "the worst viper in the heart, the first sin that ever entered the universe and [it] is the most secret and unsearchable because it is ready to mix itself with everything good."

When the leaders in the story above looked at how God was using them, they eventually came to believe that they, and not Jesus, were responsible for what was happening. *Oh,* they might have said, *it was Jesus,* but inside they probably suspected He could not have done it without them. They became like Nebuchadnezzar, king of Babylon, who looked out from his balcony one day and said to himself, "Is not this the great Babylon I have built as the royal residence, by my mighty power and for the glory of my majesty?" (Daniel 4:30, NIV).

The sin of pride can slip into anyone involved in a move of the Spirit with the purpose of bringing about division, just as it did in heaven. Pride moves you from gratitude at simply being included in something wonderful to the place where you feel you know everything about how God moves.

This can happen to anyone. Leaders who embrace the notion that they are qualified to lead without humbling themselves to remain continual receivers are fair prey for pride. Plain folks in the pews can become just as proud, particularly in relation to authority figures. I have seen members of congregations become convinced that the leaders are quenching the Holy Spirit when it is really they who are jealous of position. Something in them wants badly to be noticed. When they are asked to testify, they seize the opportunity to preach, display a gift or talk about themselves or their ministries. They rarely testify about how they were in deep need and God came to them in mercy.

We should never allow ourselves to become conceited. We should keep administering ourselves big enough doses of the fear of the Lord to realize, as Jesus said, that God could take rocks and raise up children to Abraham. He can just as easily use someone else.

Lust for Things

Another breeding ground for the Jezebel influence is lust for things. Jesus warned that distractions such as cares, worries, riches and lust uproot what God has sown and cause people to be open prey for the seduction of the enemy. The enemy will even use positive things and cause us to fixate on them instead of on Jesus' love. Revival is not about promoting our ministries or receiving personal gain. When revival comes, it produces many byproducts—including, for some, fame and financial blessing. Sometimes it is this fruit that attracts people rather than the presence of God Himself.

I believe in providing generously for God's servants, but as Elisha told his servant in so many words, "This is not a time to focus on getting rich" (see 2 Kings 5:26). Anyone who falls into the fame or money trap, as the leaders in the church I described did, may wake one awful day to realize that he or she is like Esau who sold his birthright for a single meal. Don't let that happen! Believe me, when you see Jesus, you will wish you had written Him a check for every penny you own. Just give Him control of it now; that is all He wants.

Jezebel will use the weaknesses of pride and lust to derail a move of the Spirit. Let us ask God to help us receive blessing with humility and not be taken over with insecurities that cause us to lust for money or power. If you see either of these in yourself, ask God to expose the root lie that causes you to be tempted, and then turn away from it.

SEDUCTION

A Jezebel influence can gain a foothold in a person's life, causing him to transfer deep love for the Lord onto another individual, sometimes an authority figure, all the time believing he is being spiritual. Perhaps deep inside he knows that something is wrong, but the draw is too strong. *No, it can't be,* he thinks to himself. *This affection is godly. Look at all the fruit in this person's life. Look how God is using this person whom I admire.*

During times of revival, the Holy Spirit begins to revive passion for Jesus. Sometimes people who love God have difficulty keeping the focus of their affection on "things above." Looking for someone else who loves God and who represents God to them affords them the affection they crave. It becomes more complicated when two people, especially of the opposite sex, are sympathetic to the move of the Spirit and begin to share heart to heart. Bonding takes place, sometimes followed by an unhealthy emotional attachment. This can also occur between two people of the same sex.

It is important to avoid circumstances under which such ties can develop and, if such a tie exists, to cut it before immoral behavior occurs.

In the case I mentioned at the beginning of the chapter, the leader was already vulnerable to women. This, coupled with the favor he was receiving from women in the church who were transferring affection onto him, was for him too great a temptation.

Even if there is no personal contact, even if the transference of undue affection takes place only in the fantasy realm, an individual can develop unhealthy expectations of another that cloud his or her perceptions. The person who is the object of transference can be innocent of any wrongdoing, but might be well aware of what is happening and doing nothing to stop it.

The evil spirit's purpose in this type of seduction is to distract someone from enjoying God's presence and to turn his or her gaze onto man. Sadly, some emotionally needy leaders enjoy this attention. In order to resist Jezebel on this level, keep your focus on Jesus by soaking in His presence and resist any temptation to transfer your affection to things or people here on earth.

PUSHING ASIDE THE REAL ANOINTING

The Jezebel of Elijah's day controlled Israel through fear of what she could do. When Elijah challenged the prophets of Baal on Mt. Carmel, God answered by sending fire out of heaven that consumed them and that vindicated Himself as the real God and Elijah as His servant. This divine barbecue was a picture of what happens to evil when the fire falls! The kingdom of darkness is forced to retreat.

You would think that those who witnessed this scene would forever remember that God's power is all-sufficient, but they did not—not even Elijah. We need to learn from Elijah's mistake. After God's fire falls, it is important to guard against Jezebel. We need to keep focused on Jesus and be more filled with His love than with the elation of victory. Staying in awe of Jesus diminishes the works of Satan.

After Elijah's great victory, Jezebel sent word that she planned to kill him in the next 24 hours. Suddenly he feared her more than he trusted God to protect him. He ran from her and hid, fell into depression and could not recover, even though God spoke to him personally. Soon God replaced him with Elisha and called him home.

Jezebel's power lay in her satanic ability to discourage, and it had the power to pressure even a victorious prophet into resigning. One hour Elijah was happy over the victory, and the next hour he was depressed and full of fear.

When someone in revival falls under this influence, he will manifest the same symptoms. He suddenly believes it is over and begins to fear what man can do to him. The Jezebel influence is another way of discouraging those involved in revival so they will put it aside. "What's the use?" they say. "There's no hope." In this way Satan hinders revival when it springs up, shoves aside God's anointing and tries to replace it with man-appointed authority.

Roberts Liardon, author of *God's Generals,* believes this is what happened to Evan Roberts during the Welsh revival of the early twentieth century. A woman named Jessie Penn-Lewis attached herself to the ministry and began to exert undue influence on Evan Roberts. Her knowledge of the Bible and her ability to teach impressed many, but Roberts, who already suffered from depression, fell prey to her need to control. Liardon writes that Mrs. Penn-Lewis finally convinced Evan Roberts to believe "that unless he was totally crucified to self, he was deceived. Filled with condemnation, Evan finally agreed that all the supernatural operations he had experienced couldn't have been of God."

Evan Roberts endorsed Jessie Penn-Lewis' book *War on the Saints,* which was responsible for a great quenching of the Holy Spirit, as people determined that what had happened was soulish. Many who had been converted in the Welsh revival were shocked that Roberts now opposed the invasions of the supernatural gifts of the Holy Spirit that had characterized the meetings in which they had been saved.

Although Evan Roberts saw a brief period of revival after his father's death in 1928, he spent the last years of his life quietly and died in 1951. It was as though he had become weak in the face of Jezebel.

The Fear of Man

Jezebel's husband was a weak man named Ahab who was supposed to be the real king of Israel. Biblical evidence suggests that he lived in fear of his wife and would not stand up against her idolatry. Ahab was afraid of Elijah, too. Whenever he found himself under godly influence, he swayed in the direction of the godly prophet, but whenever he was under Jezebel's influence, he could not say no to her.

In the same way, some people positioned around a man or woman with a Jezebel influence are afraid to speak up in the face of evil. Either they do not feel they have the influence or they fear it will backfire on them and they will be accused of rebellion. The fear of man gets the best of them.

Those surrounding the leader who cannot stand to see him fall create around him a protective cocoon. Their own livelihoods depend on the masquerade, so they keep it up even to the point of hypocrisy. They will lie for the leader and cover up his sins. The best they can hope for is that people will not find out.

The Jezebel influence causes others to leave quietly when they realize that the situation will not change and that they cannot continue in it. Once again it pushes the faithful to the side by discouraging them, and it replaces them with morally weak people who resemble Ahab and keep the fallen leader in power.

Revival in a local church under Jezebel's influence will cease. Sometimes God withdraws the dimension of His reviving presence from the services. This occurs only after a prolonged period of time because the Holy Spirit's desire is to keep coming. He wants more than anything to forgive and restore the people who are falling. But our Father does not want His children to be taken advantage of either.

Scripture teaches us (recall Revelation 2:20) that we are not to tolerate Jezebel. I believe that it is possible to refuse

Jezebel's influence, to find another place where God is moving in purity—such as another local church that is embracing the revival—and to walk in the spiritual dimension you have received, whether anyone else wants to or not.

Jezebel in the Pew

As I have mentioned, Jezebel is not confined to the pulpit or the boardroom; she also sits in the pew and flourishes in people who are insecure enough to look for fault in someone else. People who have the need to control others around them can create a faction and seduce the unsuspecting away from the outpouring of revival. I have heard of this happening all too often, since this move of the Spirit began, as pastors relate their heartaches to us.

When revival begins and continues for a long time in a congregation, it is a stretch for all concerned. We need to give each other a wide space to learn how to accommodate ourselves to what God is doing. Sometimes people in the pew feel threatened by the changes taking place around them. If they mistakenly feel that God will not touch them or believe the negative influences around them, they will alienate themselves from the outpouring of the Holy Spirit.

Jezebel will come and erode their simple, childlike trust in God and seduce them away from God's presence. It starts with faultfinding and negativity over what God is doing. Once they stop soaking, the focus is no longer about knowing Him but about petty grievances. They shove aside the leaders that God has anointed to make a safe place for them and sometimes they determine to take others with them. Gradually they take themselves out. They do not know that Jezebel has led them astray. If this has happened to you, you can refuse to tolerate the woman Jezebel any longer. Humble yourself and go back home.

JEZEBEL IN THE CITY

Jesus' warning about Jezebel in the book of Revelation was to the citywide church in Thyatira. The Jezebel influence, operating on a community-wide level, creates jealousy and suspicion among the leaders and prevents unity from developing. It will try to stifle the anointed leaders within the community who want to flow in the revival.

The stigma associated with revival can create such fear of being permanently ostracized that a leader begins to take his cue from others who despise it or who have been involved but are pulling out because the cost has become too great. Sometimes the conflict generated by true revival will cause a church to lose tithing members. Suppose that church is involved in a building program? The temptation is to push the revival aside.

In order not to be different, others who exert weaker influence will join in the chorus that says, "The revival is over. We need to move on." But to what? Until God brings another wave of the Spirit, all these people have to return to is performance-oriented Christianity, most of which functions solely on man-generated events and structures.

As we discussed in the first chapter, some people believe that unity brings revival. But unity is possible only when God sends a move of His Spirit. Then a common hunger brings like reactions to the presence of God. Until that moment, there will be either enough conflict or enough apathy to prevent unity. Remember, too, that there is a big difference between unity of the Spirit, which is a byproduct of revival, and "unity" of religious politics. Throughout the centuries the work of the Holy Spirit has suffered at the hands of religious politics—power in the hands of people who want to control it through various flavors of institutionalization.

Eddie Hyatt, professor of Church history at Christ for the Nations Institute in Dallas, Texas, wrote this in his book *2000 Years of Charismatic Christianity*: "In the Church, an emphasis or over-emphasis on organization always comes at the expense of the life and freedom of the Spirit." Hyatt says that "institutionalism in the early Church arose as a means of defense against persecution from the state and imposition of error from heretical sects. . . ."

One current teaching that presents a threat to the move of the Holy Spirit is the concept that within one city there are only a few main leaders. These are usually people who have achieved prominence and whose churches are large and well-institutionalized. If they have founded churches and serve them humbly, no doubt they are truly apostles. The perversion of this teaching, however, establishes them as "gatekeepers of a city." Any leader who feels that God is calling him to that city must then concern himself with pleasing the "gatekeepers" or find himself ostracized from community-wide acceptance.

In other words, anything that the Lord may want to do, including revival, would filter through these prominent ministers. If something springs up, they must oversee it. This is nothing new. It has been going on since the first century and has been responsible for quenching the Holy Spirit and "stoning the prophets" in every generation since.

What if the gatekeepers do not accept the new thing God is doing? What if they are the ones who want to quench what God is doing because it threatens their financial or power bases? Or what if they are secretly immoral? Or what if they are jealous themselves?

During this move of the Spirit it is not unusual to see Christian leaders ostracize a church in revival. Sometimes the ministers are jealous or misunderstand the way God is moving, but they condemn it and even forbid their people to go to the church that is holding renewal meetings. I have seen genuine lovers of God accused of wrong motives or even lewd and wicked behavior as rumors fly around a city. The revival's effects in that city will be compromised in the same way every move of God has been attacked in Church history. Jezebel will quench it with false authority and control.

Any pastor who has received a deposit of the reviving presence of the Lord in his or her congregation is responsible for nurturing it one hundred percent without being concerned about pleasing other leaders. He or she is not to tolerate the woman Jezebel who will try to quench with disapproval the fire that God has lit.

Let us look more closely at revival on a community-wide scale. What can be done to combat this powerful spiritual Jezebel influence and keep it from blocking revival?

COMMUNITY-WIDE UNITY

I have seen community-wide revival meetings erupt in different locations several times. This happens when various leaders are open to the revival that God is pouring out. As brothers and sisters soak in God's presence, their hearts become soft toward each other. Real relationships based on honesty undergird the revival and help sustain it. When God is in control everyone in the city who is awakening to the move of the Spirit will be welcomed into the circle and swim in the River together. They will all be "speaking the same language," and there will be no division among them.

During the spring and summer of 2000, a healing revival broke out in Stratford, Ontario. Three churches of different denominations met together for several months as God's power to heal hovered over the community. Lost people were being saved and word spread like wildfire in the community, even among unbelievers. After a period of time it seemed that God had finished what He intended to do with the churches together. It was necessary for the local pastors to carry the anointing into their own congregations.

Yet even with fruitful community-wide meetings such as those in Stratford, problems will arise. One practical difficulty comes from having a host church. This church may have to foot the utility bills, but it also generally receives financial benefits as well as the notoriety and bolstered attendance. The other churches that are called upon to help service it have to place the revival going on in their own churches on hold with no support coming in to sustain it.

Another problem arises when leaders feel compelled to join a man-generated emphasis on unity in the city when they have not been touched powerfully enough to want to change to accommodate what God is doing. In order to reach cooperation, the power level of a meeting must be reduced to the lowest common denominator. The revival is destined to be quenched.

For community-wide revival to flourish, everyone involved —especially the leaders—needs to have a common love for the way God is pouring Himself out. They must all be drinking the same new wine and be in agreement as to the boundaries. They all need to be willing to allow their wineskins to expand to contain the blessing God is pouring out.

That is why sustained revival, one that transcends a brief crusade, is usually impossible except with a local congregation. Perhaps the purpose of community-wide revival in God's eyes is to cause the outpouring to revolutionize every local congregation. Maybe God is going to send a day when we will see these community-wide problems evaporate permanently, a day when genuine, sustained unity is restored to all the members of the Body of Christ in a city, and a day when Jezebel cannot gain a foothold. Until then we must be faithful to what we know.

Paul commands us to "preserve the unity of the Spirit in the bond of peace" (Ephesians 4:3). Let us continue our study by exploring the real unity of the Spirit.

Unity and the Tower of Babel

People will often say that we must maintain unity at any cost. What we must maintain is the God-initiated unity that comes about as the result of being touched by His presence. While it is always good to love the brethren, it is humanly impossible to love them unless we abide in Him. It is, therefore, impossible to preserve man-generated unity. It will eventually fail because it is not based on revelation. No progress in the Body of Christ, including Martin Luther's Reformation, would have ever been achieved had people adopted the policy of maintaining man-generated unity at any cost.

We read in Genesis 11 what God thinks about things we build with our own attempts at unity. This is the story of the tower of Babel. The people, who all spoke the same language, got together and said, "Come, let us build ourselves a city, with a tower that reaches to the heavens" (verse 4, NIV). In other words, "Let us try to touch heaven by building something together."

They used brick instead of stone, something manmade instead of God-made, and tar for mortar, a substance that would melt in the heat. God came down to see it. He said that if He allowed them to continue, "then nothing they plan to do will be impossible for them" (verse 6, NIV). This is more than interesting when you consider that we are living in a day when such things as genetic engineering and the international space station give man the capacity to control the world and everyone in it.

At the tower of Babel, God used an unusual means to bring division so that the people would abandon what they were trying to do. He put different languages in their mouths. Suddenly, they could not understand each other. At Pentecost it is no wonder that when the Holy Spirit came, God reversed the judgment. In the upper room, everyone had a new language in his or her mouth and the bystanders could suddenly understand what was being spoken. God was ready to build His temple, the Body of Christ.

When God moves in revival, everyone who genuinely submits himself to the presence of God and receives the new deposit of the Holy Spirit that God is pouring out begins to speak differently. He uses words in a new context to describe what he "sees" internally. And then, amazingly, all those who were speaking differently suddenly understand the same language.

Revival and *presence* are words we use to define this current move of the Spirit, as well as the terms *"the River"* and *"the Blessing."* At Azusa Street the word was *Pentecost*. In the '40s and '50s, it was *Latter Rain*. Whatever God does in the future may produce new defining words.

Receiving the revelation that God is pouring out right now is what affects your speech and brings you into unity with other brethren enjoying His presence. It does not matter what denomination they were a part of or what nation they are from; suddenly they, like you, are experiencing the same dimension of God's presence and are placing the same value on it. They, too, have a deep love for God and how He is currently moving. That is what Paul meant when he wrote, "I would that you all speak the same thing and that there be no division among you."

This is also why talking to another Christian who is not having the same experience is like talking to someone who speaks another language. What has become so important to you is just not important to him or her, at least not yet.

What are we to do about cooperating with other brethren who are not "on the same page"? This is difficult. Being consumed with how God is pouring out on your life often means you do not have time to get involved with man-generated projects and events. Anything that feels like "works" will siphon your strength. While we should stop short of condemning others and cooperate when we can, I believe it is important to be wise about where you spend your time and "do only those things you see the Father doing." What are you hungry to do?

You can certainly pray for others in your city to experience what God has graciously poured on you through none of your own effort. Ask God to come upon them, too, and be ready to flow with them when He does.

The real unity of the Spirit is a Pentecostal finding himself lying on the floor under the power and presence of God, then coming to beside a Roman Catholic who has just had the same sort of powerful experience. The judgment of the tower of Babel is suddenly reversed. They have a common experience and vocabulary that describe how God is touching them.

With the charismatic renewal starting in the 1960s, the Holy Spirit created unity among people from every imaginable denomination who were receiving the baptism of the Holy Spirit and speaking in tongues. Hundreds of thousands of believers gathered in places like St. Louis and Pittsburgh to worship together and celebrate their unity. While some of these ducked once again into their denominational holes, it was wonderful nonetheless to sense the heaven-sent unity of the Spirit that drew individuals into those meetings; charismatics and Pentecostals worldwide now number 500 million. This renewal was a foreshadowing of the non-denominational Kingdom of God come to earth.

Unity and Denominational Fences

Another strategy of the enemy to destroy unity in revival attacks people who crave the security of too much organization.

It happens like this. As revival progresses, people who are enjoying its blessings often find themselves expelled from groups that do not share their enthusiasm. Sometimes people and churches feel orphaned by these circumstances.

They love the newly created unity of the Spirit but they also like the security that comes from having a well-recognized organization backing them. They then build their own group structure.

If care is not taken to stop the impulse to build something man-generated, they will have another "tower of Babel" on their hands. Exclusivity can develop from the "them and us" mentality that comes from the rejection they have experienced. Then, and often without being conscious of doing so, they reduce all of what God is doing into a rigid doctrine. Now in order to experience the revival, outsiders must become part of their group and adopt their doctrines and practices.

Still another difficulty arises when those who have never submitted to the new anointing the revival brings attach themselves to the new and attempt to control it either by lowering the common denominator of Holy Spirit power or by forms of political maneuvering.

In heaven we will see everything clearly and no divisions will exist among us, but man has a tendency to want to know where we are going and where we are not going. It is hard to live in an open setting where things keep changing.

God sees the Church as a living thing, a relational group, and even sees the Church in heaven and the part of her still on earth as one group: the Body. Man's view falls so far short. We close the circle and institutionalize revival to make it our own. We place organization around it and then eventually take control once again. Hierarchies develop and hurdles now surround a dimension of God's presence.

These are not, of course, the hurdles that God sometimes places around Himself to test people's motives. These are hurdles that man devises in the form of legalistic rules. Rigidity institutionalizes revival through rule-making and policy development. I believe it is good to try to surround what God is doing with as few rules as possible. Otherwise one move of God winds up rejecting the next. Sadly, as we will see in a moment, this happened in this move of the Spirit when the Holy Spirit broke out in Toronto.

HANDLING OPPOSITION TO UNITY

I wish I could say that everyone in the Church is happy when God moves in revival; they are not. Keeping the fire lit also means learning to expect and deal with opposition or it will quench the fire in you and in your city.

For everyone who thinks that revival always brings unity, I have news for you, and it is not good. For some reason the power of God in revival always generates controversy. The Toronto Blessing and the Father's Day Outpouring in Pensacola as well as other revival-related ministries have been sorely castigated by church people, some of whom have carried their complaints to national media outlets. They have frightened thousands away from its blessings.

Every revival has had its detractors. While the detractors eventually fade into obscurity, those who were faithful stewards of what God gave them "shine like the stars forever and ever," as the angel told Daniel.

Sometimes opposition to revival leads a denomination to expel a congregation from its fellowship. Such was the case with the Association of Vineyard Churches: It expelled its congregation located in Toronto. Late in 1995, the Reverend John Wimber, founder and leader of the Association of Vineyard Churches, flew to Toronto for his second visit since the outpouring had begun almost two years before. This time he called Toronto's staff together and gave his ultimatum. Toronto, in his mind, had ceased to be enough like the Vineyard model to remain in the fellowship.

He cited several reasons, which included the way Toronto prayed for people, by asking the crowds to stand in prayer lines, and what he believed to be a focus on prophecy and on the outward manifestations. He expressed concern that what was happening in Toronto was not a revival but a renewal, which he believed was different, and that they were not focusing on evangelism.

Except for praying in prayer lines, the rest of his reasons were neither true then nor true today. John Arnott had a choice: either stop conducting the revival in the manner it had come and in the way God was blessing it or leave the Vineyard. Although he did not want to, he chose to leave.

Today John and Carol Arnott have met several times with Vineyard leaders and are at peace with them. Vineyard leaders and members of their churches frequently attend meetings in Toronto to receive God's blessings. John Wimber is now deceased, but much of the genetic code that God used in this move of the Spirit came from Wimber's creative, anointed thoughts—even the prayer "Come, Holy Spirit." One leader in England told me that he could not understand John Wimber's objections to Toronto. He said that the meetings he had had with Wimber in the '80s had been graced with much more violent manifestations than had come with the Toronto Blessing. Many believe that Wimber's objections would never have been raised had he been healthy enough to observe more closely what was going on in Toronto.

Whatever the real reasons, the division that Satan meant for evil the Lord used for good. Dropping the denominational fence only gave Toronto a wider sphere of influence. Thousands continue to come from all over the world from every sector of the Body of Christ, including Vineyard churches. As I mentioned earlier, to date more than three and one-half million people have come through their doors to receive the blessings of the outpouring.

Determined to learn from the past, Toronto has begun a new fellowship of churches called Partners in Harvest, based on relational rather than hierarchical organization. No one is "over" anyone else and the purpose is still to spread the fire of the revival in local churches.

God has given grace to Pensacola, as of this writing, to stay within the Assembly of God denomination and enjoy its blessing. Granted, not all Assemblies churches agree that what is happening in Pensacola is a true revival.

What if Toronto had chosen to stop the meetings? How many people would not have been saved or healed? How much fruit would have been lost?

THE TRIP TO UNITY

I believe that the path to unity is exemplified best in the Old Testament character of Joseph. Although as we saw earlier he struggled with pride, he was his father's favorite son. His jealous brothers took from him his only sign of favor, his multi-colored coat, and threw him into a pit. They almost murdered him but sold him into slavery instead.

For more than twenty years God watched over Joseph in Egypt even through false accusations and a term in prison. Finally his prophetic gift made a way for him and brought him before the Pharaoh of Egypt. Overnight Joseph rose out of prison as God exalted him. As his prophecies came to pass and he helped Egypt through its seven-year famine, he was amazed one day to see all his brothers bowing at his feet. They did not know who he was, but Joseph knew them. After a period where he tested their character, he revealed to them who he really was.

His trip to unity led him through rejection, slavery, prison and a twenty-year sojourn in a foreign land until God vindicated him and restored him to his brothers. During this time, Joseph may have longed for his relationships, but he let his dream die.

People who give themselves to a move of the Spirit will often suffer great persecution from others in the Body of Christ because they, like Joseph, are stepping into a forerunner position. I have heard many people say how they want to be on the "cutting edge." However, the life of Joseph shows what it costs to live on the cutting edge.

Keep Hold of the Blessing

So how are we to react in the face of disunity? Charles Finney believed that revivals could not be destroyed from the outside but only from within. Keeping your heart pure by continuing to forgive will make you ready to receive those who have hurt you if they experience a change of heart. If others reject you, bless them and turn the other cheek. Sometimes you may have to flee and find safe cover, but if you keep forgiving, one day you may look out as Joseph did and see them humbly coming back.

Revival will create new relationships, too. Preserve them by genuinely loving people. This is only possible as you keep soaking in God's presence. As you keep beholding Him, you will keep a soft heart that is ready to change. You do not have to fear the Jezebel influence either, as long as you stay in awe of God. Fixing your eyes on Jesus will keep your motives free from greed, lust and self-promotion. As others focus on Jesus, too, you will find your friendships maturing and you will be able to preserve the unity the Holy Spirit has created.

God does not want you to elevate the second commandment above the first, falling into the fear of man that makes you try to place people above God. Never sacrifice what God is pouring out to stay in so-called unity with people who do not love the moving of the Spirit. This is what it means to "take up your cross and follow Jesus."

Is the glory of His presence not worth the sacrifice of your reputation and sometimes your relationships? It needs to be if you are to remain a good steward of the mystery of revival. Sacrificing your reputation to keep hold of the blessing will ultimately result in others around you being able to experience it, too, maybe even those who are rejecting you now.

Eight

Getting Back
into the River

Stephen Thompson used to play defensive tackle for the New York Jets during the heyday of Joe Namath. He even has a Super Bowl ring and flashes it occasionally if someone tries to intimidate him. But tackling the problem of staying in the River proved to be an even greater challenge.

After his days as a pro football player Stephen and his wife, Starla, entered the ministry. He became pastor of a church near Seattle, Washington, in the International Church of the Foursquare Gospel, a Pentecostal denomination founded by Aimee Semple McPherson, the famous flamboyant woman evangelist of the 1920s and '30s. The denomination's Pentecostal roots, however, did not seem to prepare the members of Stephen's church for this current move of the Spirit.

Stephen and Starla realized they needed a fresh touch from God and made their way to the outpouring in Toronto.

There they were overcome with the presence of God. He touched them in such a powerful way that they determined never again to do things at church the way they had always done them.

Once back home they instituted a Friday night renewal meeting where people came to soak and enjoy the blessings God was pouring out. Many of their members dived into the River, eager to experience all God had for them. Then the trouble began.

Dissenting factions started to oppose the leaders of the church, and within a year the church was facing a full-scale split. "It seemed as though everyone was leaving," Stephen recalls. And those who stayed were grieving over the loss of their friends. Although the church had problems before the renewal started, the focus of gossip about the turmoil quickly latched onto the church's participation in the renewal. Stephen 's ability to lead was called into question, and within a few months more than half of their congregation of 830 members left.

At that point Stephen and Starla were so discouraged that they let go of the renewal. They stopped the Friday night meetings and tried to return everything to the way it had been before the outpouring had started, working to please God with a good church program.

"We began to question everything we had seen," Stephen recalls. "When the church split started, we wondered if we were seeing bad fruit. Why had all this happened when the Holy Spirit was supposed to create unity in the fellowship?"

As time went by, however, the people who remained with them remained loyal to the renewal, too, and Stephen and Starla grew hungry again. They made another pilgrimage to Toronto. When they saw that God was still moving and that He had no intention of withdrawing His love and blessing, the Thompsons desired revival more than ever. But they wondered how they could ever bring their flock back into the River.

Stephen invited his friend Brad Davis, another Foursquare pastor, to speak at their family summer camp. Brad's church in Fresno, California, has been flowing in the renewal since 1994 and has become a watering hole in central California.

Brad began to preach about the Kingdom of God and exhorted Stephen 's church not to try to go back to the way they had been before renewal. The power of God broke out again at the camp. People who had come for "camp as usual" went home on fire. They began to experience a renewed love for Jesus. It seemed that God was dressing the wounds left by the split.

This time Stephen talked with Brad about how to keep the blessing. He never wanted to lose it again. How could he encourage the Holy Spirit to keep touching the flock the Lord had entrusted to him?

WHERE TO START

Let's examine what Brad—and God—told Stephen. It is good advice for anyone, not just pastors.

WELCOME THE PRESENCE OF GOD

"The renewal is the presence of God and it's to die for," Brad said. He is right. We need to be careful how we label what God is doing. The way we label something directly affects what we receive from it. If we believe it to be nothing, we will likely receive nothing. However, if we recognize it as a major outpouring of the Holy Spirit, we will likely enter into it and treasure it.

When you realize that God has given you something very precious, you are more likely to cherish it. When you cherish something, you give it a prominent place because of its priceless value.

Stephen and Starla returned to the deeds they were doing when the River first came to their church. These were not works-oriented programs; rather, they were deeds directed by the Holy Spirit. They amounted to spending time in God's presence, waiting on Him and absorbing His love, watching Him initiate acts of power and then cooperating with Him.

Because the renewal is the presence of God, Brad counceled Stephen to put everything on the table including all the old ways of "doing church." Brad advised: "Even if something gave the appearance of producing fruit, we can develop an elevated view of what it really produced." We need to let go of old ways so they will not interfere with the new.

Stephen and Starla listened. They began by restoring the Friday night renewal meeting. In order for the church to get into the River, the people needed to be able to receive prayer. They invited the Holy Spirit to move any way He wanted upon the congregation; many people had lost heart because of the church split. Stephen began to pray for people asking the Holy Spirit to renew and touch them.

God came powerfully. He touched the people with healing miracles and renewed their spiritual strength.

Stephen may not have realized it, but he did what Jesus said to do when you realize you have left your first love: "Remember the height from which you have fallen! Repent [which means "go back"] and do the things you did at first" (Revelation 2:5, NIV). By far the principal "thing" is lingering in the presence of God enjoying His love.

Start Soaking Again

Brad told Stephen, "You have to start soaking again in God's presence and teach your people to soak, too."

As Stephen and Starla started soaking and experiencing the love of God again, they wanted everyone in the congregation to feel God's love. And people began to respond.

This, of all the evidences of revival, has meant more to Stephen and Starla than anything else. Services are not about ceremonies or a particular order of worship but about experiencing the presence of God who does not want to be limited to a church bulletin. In fact, as they have begun to re-invite the Holy Spirit to come and take over, they, too, have found that He comes even when they are not in church.

Stephen said, for instance, that he faces anxiety about going to the dentist. During a recent visit, while sitting in the dentist's chair undergoing a routine checkup, he suddenly sensed the presence of the Lord in the room. He began to smile. Experiencing God's presence at a moment when he usually felt anxious was so soothing that he fell asleep. The dentist had never seen anyone anesthetized by the presence of God before.

Stephen says that the sense of God's love is greater now that they have gotten back into the River than it was the first time they experienced revival. The congregation is growing in its love for God, which is the true purpose of church and ministry in the first place.

All this newfound love for Jesus is producing fruit, including the ministry of helping take the River to Africa. Stephen says, "Intimacy with God is the cause of fruit production. We are in transition from being a program-oriented church to a Presence-oriented church."

Set Love as a Priority

Last summer Stephen and Starla took a three-month-long sabbatical. His assistants took over the responsibilities of the church; by this time they were too busy soaking in the glory to notice that their pastor and his wife were taking some needed days off!

During this time, the Lord Himself spoke to Stephen about rearranging his priorities. The first thing God said was not surprising: "Love Me first." The Lord gave specific instructions concerning how He wanted to be loved: He told Stephen to give Him his mornings.

Prior to this, Stephen and Starla's mornings had been a rush to get to the church and start handling the details of the day. The Lord told him that during these mornings with Him they were to spend time personally soaking in God's love, doing nothing but letting God touch them and enjoying Him. Out of their renewed communion with God, they began to fall in love with Jesus again and with one another.

Then God said, "Love your wife until she feels loved." Like many husbands he thought he was already doing that, but the key was "until she feels loved." *After all,* Stephen thought, *what good is revival unless it is happening at home?* Stephen started treating Starla the way he did when he was courting her before they were married. A river of new love started pouring into their marriage.

Then God said, "Love your children and your grandchildren until they feel loved." Stephen wondered how many details would have to be set aside at church to accomplish this, but he knew that obedience to God would be worth more to Him than sacrifice, so he decided to do this, too.

"If you do these things," God told Stephen, "by the time you are seventy years old, you will be going seventy miles per hour!" Stephen is in his fifties now. Before he got back in the River he had felt internally weary, drained of any motivation to continue. After six months of obeying the Lord, he knows he has found the secret of continuous personal revival: soaking in God and obeying the simple things He tells you to do.

This renewed love is having an effect on the congregation. Not only are they happy to see their pastor refreshed and enjoying God and his family, but they appreciate having a "new" pastor who has moved aside his manmade agenda and oversees the River as it refreshes the thirsty sheep in the fold. Stephen says that ministry is now far easier because it more closely resembles what Jesus designed it to be in the first place.

Go into the River Together

In addition to pursuing the presence of God personally, Stephen took more of Brad's advice: "Don't try to go it alone."

Brad told him to join others who are soaking constantly in the River and not to be bound by denominational lines. This would encourage Stephen and his staff that they were not in this alone, that other pastors all over the world love the River of God's presence, too. It would also "stoke the fire" that God was re-igniting in the congregation, providing another form of validation for those who were learning to trust and open up to the Holy Spirit.

Stephen invited members of the Toronto itinerant team and other pastors whose churches are being revolutionized by what God is doing to come to Seattle. Their congregation sets aside special weekends to focus on the renewal. As congregants hear testimonies and teaching from other ministers who are also soaking in the presence of God and encouraging their congregations to do so, they realize the value of what God is sending. Signs and wonders have begun to increase in the congregation, causing deeper hunger for God.

Stephen's church is rediscovering the secret of the early Church's ongoing revival. There is a direct correlation between being in awe of God's presence and continuing to see Him work: "Everyone kept feeling a sense of awe; *and* many wonders and signs were taking place through the apostles" (Acts 2:43, emphasis added).

Stephen says today, "We'll never go back to the way we were before. This is just too wonderful. It's about continually experiencing the Father's love. Before, I thought it was about seeing the outward manifestations. Perhaps I focused too much on seeing outward signs and whether or not there was enough fruit. Now I'm being drawn by His love. It's the most important thing."

COMING BACK TO HIS PRESENCE

What really happened to Stephen and Starla is a three-thousand-year-old story with a twenty-first-century twist. It happened to none other than King David, Israel's most beloved king, when he first tried to bring the Ark of the Covenant back to Jerusalem from its storage place in the border town of Kiriath-jearim.

I would like to spend some time with this story because it speaks to anyone who has felt discouraged when God's presence in revival seems to create more problems at first than solutions. Have you felt like setting down the blessing of revival? You are not alone. David did, too, at first, until he learned this lesson. It is found in 2 Samuel 6 and 1 Chronicles 13.

For more than twenty years during the reign of Saul, the Ark of the Covenant, the central piece of furniture in Moses' tabernacle and Israel's most prized antique, had been kept away from public view. It was holed away in the home of Abinadab the priest, who had two sons, Uzzah and Ahio.

The first official act of David's administration was to bring the Ark back to the center of Israel's religious life. But the attempt failed. As the celebration commenced, the oxen pulling the cart stumbled on a threshing floor and the Ark nearly slid off. Uzzah, serving as one of the oxcart drivers, reached out his hand to steady it. There was something about his touch that God did not like. Maybe it was disrespect or even apathy, but instantly, as if stunned by an unseen blow, Uzzah fell dead.

In a fit of anger, David withdrew from God. "How then shall God's Ark come home to me?" he cried. It was as if God was saying, "Get Me down from here. I don't want to ride like this."

Not knowing what else to do, David stopped the parade and ordered a bystander named Obed-edom, a resident of Goliath's old hometown of Gath, to take it home. The Bible is not clear about Obed-edom. His name means "servant of Edom," but he had been living in a Philistine city far removed from the center of Israelite religion and commerce. Maybe he is like many of us who are destined to be lovers of God; we have just never seen enough of Him to want to get that close.

For three months the Ark of God rested in the home of an ordinary man, not a priest, not even a Hebrew, but a Philistine—a man of a race of people despised by Israel. When the Ark was previously in the home of Abinadab and his family, it resided with priests who obviously were not very much humbled and amazed at what they had in their "closet." Abinadab apparently never taught Uzzah and Ahio what would happen if they touched the Ark the wrong way. I get the impression that they did not seem to care.

But now it was in the home of a man who knew one thing: He was to respect and honor the thousand-year-old prized antiquity that represented the presence of God to Israel, a God that Obed-edom knew little about. It is likely that Obed-edom was afraid to touch the Ark. After what had happened to Uzzah, he probably put a little distance between it and himself. Maybe he sat just looking at it, possibly remembering the stories of the fiascoes the Philistines had experienced when God's golden box had fallen into their hands. Although we do not know what went on at Obed-edom's home, we know that God liked the way He was treated there.

We know this because during the three months that Obed-edom kept the Ark, God blessed everything in his house, even to the extended relatives. The women conceived children; the flocks and herds multiplied. Scripture says that the rewards of the fear of the Lord are "riches, honor and life." It was all happening at Obed-edom's house in ways so obvi-ous as to set him apart. People knew it was because of one thing: God's presence in his living room.

I wonder if David woke up one morning and wondered how many people were dead at Obed-edom's house. Surely by now, God would have finished them off, too, as he had done with Uzzah. He sent word to find out. To his surprise, David found Obed-edom's house loaded with blessings and prosperity of every kind.

Now David wanted the Ark, too. He was learning hard les-sons about being a faithful, humble steward of the presence of God. Because he saw what was happening with Obed-edom, David was inspired to try again to bring the presence of God back into the center of their lives. This time David got it right. He told the priests to get ready to carry the Ark. He explained, "We didn't seek God about it before, and He burst out against us because the priests weren't carrying it."

Getting ready to carry the Ark was not easy. It had not been properly carried in nearly twenty years. The priests who were sons of the last people to carry it may have had to look it up in the scrolls of the Law of Moses. They had to cleanse them-selves, be anointed with sacrificial blood and holy oil and don their linen ephods.

David wanted to join in. He had waited for years for this moment. He did not care if anyone knew who the king of Israel was that day. He wanted no distinction between him-self and the priests. He only wanted to rejoice as he returned to the presence of God. So the king of Israel put on a linen ephod, too.

Then the festivities began. The procession was assembled and the musicians found their places. The consecrated priests took their assigned positions beside the golden box with cherubim on the top. They put their hands on the poles and lifted the Ark off the ground and onto their shoulders, and for the first time in two generations God was where He wanted to be: in intimate contact with His people.

God was so happy that He let them carry Him down the road. David was so happy that he started dancing and could not stop. I think he was once again feeling the presence of God as he had felt it as a boy in the shepherd's field. People could not believe how hard he danced, but he became for all time the model of a leader's receptivity, a go-for-it, unabashed participator and not a spectator.

After six paces, the priests stopped and offered sacrifices because God was with them this time. They had learned from their failure and had discovered the eternal secret of walking with the Lord: moving with God, not trying to move God. Then the parade resumed. God seemed to be happy being carried next to the faces of the priests who had taken the trouble to touch Him.

As I visualize the priests carrying the Ark, I can imagine God saying to all of us, "I know I'm a lot of trouble and I sometimes do things you don't understand, but all I want is to be close to you if you want to take the time to be close to Me."

Maybe that is what we need to realize. We cannot "move" God with anything but our desire for Him because His presence is so wonderful.

OPENING THE WAY FOR OTHERS TO GO AFTER THE PRESENCE OF GOD

In all this celebration, the man who had looked after God's Ark was not left out of the picture. Something had happened to this obscure man of uncertain origin but certain destiny. Because God had honored Obed-edom with abundant blessings, David honored him, too. He grafted him into the priesthood and appointed him and 68 of his relatives to worship God before the Ark night and day alongside the Levitical musicians.

Until that moment only one person, the high priest, on only one day, the Day of Atonement, was allowed access to the presence of God in the tabernacle. Because of what happened to Obed-edom David instituted a new order; it opened the way to the presence of God for those who wanted to worship Him as their chief occupation. A Gentile from Gath found himself included in this elite group.

A thousand years later the Jerusalem counsel convened with an urgent question: Should Gentiles be allowed into the Church? In answer James quoted Amos 9:11–12 to the other apostles: "'After these things I will return, and I will rebuild the tabernacle of David which has fallen, and I will rebuild its ruins, and I will restore it, so that the rest of mankind may seek the LORD . . . ,' says the LORD" (Acts 15:16–18). What Gentiles were in the tabernacle of David? "The remnant of Edom and all the nations who are called by My name" (Amos 9:12).

Had the prophet Amos and now James seen the life of Obed-edom in prophetic shadow of things to come? Probably, because the rewards Obed-edom received were unprecedented.

THE REWARDS OF OBED-EDOM

Because Obed-edom had taken care of God's presence, God increased his responsibilities. David pitched a tent near his palace for the Ark of the Covenant and set Obed-edom as gatekeeper. He decided who went in and who stayed out. Apparently, watching the presence of God had given him an intuitive sense about what God wanted and did not want. He did not want apathy; He wanted honor and respect. He did not want business as usual; He wanted awe. He did not want a place; He wanted the only place.

Then God increased Obed-edom's responsibilities again. David assigned to the house of Obed-edom the honor of guarding the treasury of the house of God. This seems a logical step to me because once you have tasted of His presence and He has become your only treasure, material possessions have their proper place. Compared to God, they mean nothing other than a greater means of blessing others.

The house of Obed-edom held this honored position until the destruction of the Temple by the Babylonians. Later when the Temple was restored, Scripture says that the leaders brought out the treasures of the house of God *with* Obed-edom. These stewards had been faithful unto death guarding what had been entrusted to them. God made sure that this noble act received mention. While others abandoned the house of God before the Babylonian captivity, the house of Obed-edom kept faithful to their posts.

Why am I mentioning this now in a chapter about getting back in the River? Because just as Obed-edom's stewardship encouraged David to return to God's presence, so it inspires other people to make the risk themselves today. It is a push-all-your-poker-chips-to-the-middle-of-the-table commitment. When someone displays this kind of honor before God, he is fulfilling his destiny as a royal priest, "teaching people the difference between the sacred and the ordinary." It inspires other people to return to the River.

For the past eight years I have been simultaneously enjoying what God is doing and praying for more of it. I believe God is about to inundate us with the "more" we have been praying for. I hope in that moment He says to me, "Well done. You treasured what I gave you and invested it, now I will give you more."

WHERE IS REVIVAL NOW?

People sometimes ask me, "Whatever happened to the Toronto Blessing?" Simply by asking the question those individuals show that they have walked away from the River. Maybe they left out of discouragement when the presence of God brought a church split or division between friends. It is easy to understand.

But there are people like Stephen and Starla all over the world who are taking another look. Maybe they miss the sense of God's presence that they see in churches that would not let Him go. In any event, they are finding the courage to return. And God will come and come more powerfully than they ever imagined because, like King David, they have learned the difficult lesson of stewardship of the presence of God and they will never let go again.

If you were once in the River but have gotten out for some reason, you can go back. Being humble enough to admit your need is the first step. It is not easy, but Stephen and Starla did it and so has everyone else who began to long for what they let go of. Like King David, they are finding where they set God down and returning to the blessing of a lifetime, maybe an eternal lifetime!

Now we will look at what it takes to guard what you have been given, to keep the springs of revival.

Nine

Keeping the Springs of Revival

No piece of property, especially in a desert, is worth much without water. Finding a well instantly increases land value. In the same way, God is changing the face of the world by causing wells of revival to spring up in communities all over the world, in fulfillment of Isaiah 41:17–18:

> "The afflicted and needy are seeking water, but there is none, and their tongue is parched with thirst; I, the LORD, will answer them Myself, as the God of Israel I will not forsake them. I will open rivers on the bare heights, and springs in the midst of the valleys; I will make the wilderness a pool of water and the dry land fountains of water."

Within a year after the outpouring started, God turned our own congregation into a watering hole in the Greater Pittsburgh area. This is how it happened.

At every meeting we kept soaking in the presence of God, encouraging everyone to continue receiving prayer. Many of us lingered in God's presence at church and at home, too.

When this happens, the outward manifestations often grow stronger, and the signature inward sign becomes a strong love for the Lord, which also continues to increase.

After I finished the manuscript of *The River Is Here* in 1995, Jane Campbell, my editor at Chosen Books, sent it to Toronto hoping that John Arnott would review it. At that time I had been to Toronto ten times but had never met the Arnotts. In January 1996 we found a message on the answering machine: "We want to talk to Melinda. We're reading her book and we love it. Please have her call us back."

I recognized the ingenuous voice of John Arnott. Nervously I returned the call.

"We want to come to Pittsburgh," he said.

At the time Bill and I were engaged in combined meetings with other churches. I invited them to join us. But what he really wanted to do, he said, was come down to our church— "just to soak and see what's happening down there."

So we set a time. And what was originally supposed to be an intimate soaking time with the Arnotts for our congregation quickly got out of hand. Word got around, and before long we realized we would never have enough room in our small sanctuary for all those who planned to attend; so we booked a hotel ballroom.

At the time our congregation had fewer than one hundred people, and none of us was rich enough to cover that kind of expense. So we knew that if God did not move, we would face nothing short of putting a *for sale* sign in front of the church building the morning after the meetings!

Meanwhile, we had canceled our traditional Wednesday night meeting and had begun holding a Friday night renewal meeting. It generally drew fewer than fifty people. There were nights when we wondered if anyone would show up. But one Friday night one of our members had a sister visiting from Ohio who was deaf in one ear because of a childhood accident. During the worship time at the beginning of the service, the sister came to the front and knelt down. A few moments passed. Suddenly she jumped up and began to scream, "I can hear! I can hear!" This sovereign healing gave us courage to continue with our Friday night renewal meetings.

On the first night with the Arnotts a crowd began to line up outside the ballroom. When everyone was seated, more than sixteen hundred people from the greater Pittsburgh area packed the room, including seventy pastors. The Holy Spirit fell and springs of water flowed out to the hungry and thirsty in our city.

After that weekend, our Friday night renewal meeting was bursting at the seams. People became instantly addicted to this new dimension of God's presence. It seemed that the Lord had opened a wellspring and wanted us to tend it.

Since 1996 the hungry and thirsty from all over Pennsylvania, Ohio, West Virginia and even other countries have come to the Friday night renewal meetings to soak in God's presence on our church's red carpet.

God is calling every congregation that experiences this blessing to stewardship, trusting it with His treasure. I do not know about you, but we have discovered that in order to guard this spring, we have had to do three things: know the value of what we have been given; keep its purity; and prevent anything from blocking its flow.

Let's look at each of these.

KNOW THE VALUE OF WHAT YOU HAVE

The greatest principle of stewardship is knowing the value of what has been entrusted to your care. I have learned this in various ways. The most visually powerful example came on a trip to the jewel house in the Tower of London.

I am as American as they come, but my first experience on the moving walkway past the jewel cases took my breath away. Glittering under the lights were England's golden crowns, which have adorned the heads of the nation's sovereigns since the 1600s and which are encrusted with thousands of diamonds and other precious stones.

On top of the monarch's scepter is the 531-carat Star of Africa diamond, the largest cut diamond in the world. The second-largest diamond is displayed in the Imperial State Crown, 371 carats amid its more than 2,800 other diamonds. The solid golden punch bowl is big enough to bathe in. We are talking major jewelry here.

"How much are they worth?" I asked one of the Yeoman Warders.

"We don't know," he said. "There's nothing with which to compare them."

How valuable to you is experiencing the presence of God? Is it incomparable? Would you inconvenience yourself for years to guard it and give it away? Would you die for it? If you are a pastor, the question of whether or not revival takes hold in your congregation and stays very long depends on your answer. Indeed, the churches that still carry this blessing after several years are the places where the pastors were the most desperate and where they continue to place the highest value on how God is moving. They are "receivers" themselves who are not ashamed to soak in God's presence, even in front of their congregations.

Every individual must recognize that the deposit of God's presence received in this outpouring is priceless.

One of the most powerful services I have attended in Toronto was the anniversary service in January 1997. Dr. R. T. Kendall, an American who pastors Westminster Chapel, an evangelical church in the Westminster area of London, was speaking—or trying to. For several minutes, one of the most eloquent evangelical speakers of our time stood speechless in the pulpit, fumbling for words. He tried several times to launch into his prepared message on the topic of discouragement.

The reaction from the thousands of people present was appreciative, sympathetic laughter. They thought Dr. Kendall was being stopped by the Holy Spirit from speaking, as a number of speakers have been affected that way.

After about fifteen minutes, Dr. Kendall said, "I believe I have the wrong message." From that moment he began to preach in power about Christ suffering reproach outside the gate of Jerusalem, and calling us to accompany Him outside the gate and suffer with Him.

The message lasted ten minutes. When he finished, ministers who felt they had compromised the previous move of God for their reputations flooded the altar. They wanted to embrace any stigma that might come with this new move of the Spirit.

The fact is, there *is* a stigma attached to revival. In the previous revival, the stigma involved the gifts of the Spirit. And in this move of the Spirit, as we have seen, God has placed a fence of embarrassing outward manifestations around His presence.

Anything that creates a stigma flies in the face of the status quo and upsets religious systems. Not everyone receives revival; some feel threatened by it and actually persecute it. In fact, I have mentioned the mysterious but well-documented historical observation: The opponents of a revival are frequently the ones who were touched in the previous move of God.

In order to suffer reproach "outside the gate," you must be more interested in what God has for you in revival than in the distractions the devil will hurl at you. These distractions can take the form of ridicule, opposition, church splits, loss of friends and finances. Sometimes things begin to look bleak before they look better. If a pastor sees revival as a means of fulfilling his own agenda, increasing membership, building a building or soothing inner insecurities, either the church will not be able to move into revival or else whatever God does will be short-lived. If someone in the pew sees the effects of what God is doing as beneath his dignity, he will be unwilling to suffer the stigma associated with it.

God has appointed the office of pastor in a local church for the protection and nurture of the flock. God does not violate those purposes in revival. He knocks on the pastor's door and involves him in the revival. For a church to embrace revival fully, it must mean everything to the pastor personally. In order for a church to stay in the River, its minister must remain so in awe of what God is doing that no other treasure comes close. He needs to keep on soaking or else, like everyone else, he will lose sight of the value of what he has been given.

Many people wonder if their pastors will embrace this new move of the Spirit. I believe God has prepared pastors all over the globe for the revival that is now in progress and the other phases to come. He has made them hungry enough to humble themselves to go somewhere to be touched, and although they are called to oversee the flocks, God is helping them learn to release tight controls so that the Holy Spirit can move.

If your church is not embracing revival because of the stigma attached to it, and yet you are hungry for it, you will need to feed yourself elsewhere. You must follow the hunger God has given you with the godly wisdom He also supplies. If the people in your church are happy, let them be, but follow your spiritual appetite. If you grow so hungry that you know your traditions have to go, you may need to change churches. Be gracious about it, but find another church in your area that is welcoming revival.

The charismatic renewal lost momentum because so many people sat waiting for their churches to enter the mainstream of what God was doing. Once eager for God, they missed out on the blessed results of revival because they mistakenly believed that He would one day revolutionize their churches or denominations. They waited for nearly two decades, which meant that their children grew up without being exposed to supernatural Christianity. God never revives entire denominations. He is not restricted by denominationalism but works without manmade limitations.

Keeping the New Wine Pure

When the Toronto renewal began in 1994, I heard many people use a phrase I have repeated several times. After being touched by God, they said that "this is to die for." They meant this literally. They were lifted into a realm they had never seen, and which had not been seen by the majority of the Church throughout the centuries. These brothers and sisters would pay whatever it cost.

Yet not every one of those touched by God continued in renewal. Some of the same people who yearned at first for the treasure returned within two years to business as usual. They threw aside the irreplaceable blessing they were offered. Why?

In some cases those who gulped the springs of renewal were simply "old wine" drinkers. Jesus talked about people who, after tasting the new wine, put it down and say, "The old is good enough." In other words, "What I want in my relationship with Jesus is being satisfied by the wine He has already poured out, the previous move of God, the former glory. I'm not thirsty for anything more."

In this way God seems to bring individuals and whole congregations to the "new wine bottle" to test them. He gives things of great value to people to give them a chance at stewardship.

The most expressive example I can think of is Judas' reaction to the precious presence of Jesus. The Lord had called Judas to be a disciple, and he would have been an eternal apostle had he not cast the privilege aside.

Judas did not really know who Jesus was. He was not a worshiper. When Mary bathed Jesus' feet in expensive perfume, Judas begrudged the Lord the act of worship. The disciple's response to this emotionally uncomfortable scene revealed his heart. He thought the money should have been spent on the poor. It sounds noble, but by comparing the monetary value of the perfume with its immeasurable symbolic value in anointing Jesus for His death, Judas failed the first lesson of stewardship: knowing the value of what you have been given.

How often have I heard people say that soaking in God's presence is not as valuable as witnessing or ministering to the poor! But I believe this concept is erroneous. It is the intimate presence of God that must fuel our work, or everything we do will burn in the judgment.

While aged wine may taste better, I am told that new wine is often more potent, causing the one who drinks it to become inebriated more quickly. This is the image Jesus chose to describe the powerful effect of the Holy Spirit on someone who receives Him. Jesus does not want us to be satisfied with what pleases our own tastes, but with what will radically affect us, both inwardly and outwardly. Church history testifies that every revival restores an experience with God that we need. Why would we refuse what God is giving us? Surely He sends it because He thinks we need it.

"Old wine" drinkers can threaten a move of the Spirit because they are unwilling to make the radical changes necessary to accommodate it. They create a rigid structure around God and are not flexible enough to change. In order to hold onto their fabrications, they will either reject revival or try to mix the old with the new and pollute the streams.

In other words, to continue in our stewardship, we must abandon our own agendas once we recognize the treasure in our midst, or else they will pollute the flow.

How do we do that?

Agendas vs. Revival

We start by realizing that one of the greatest threats to personal and corporate revival is the rivalry between a human-generated agenda (the old wineskin) and God-initiated revival (the new wine). The human agenda defines the parameters of corporate church life and defiles the springs of revival. These agendas usually proceed out of the natural understanding of sincere hearts that are hoping to serve God in a pleasing yet sometimes impatient way.

The well-known story of God's promise of a son to Abraham is a classic example. God told Abraham twenty years before Isaac was born that he would eventually be the father of many nations. When seven years passed and God seemed in no particular hurry to act, Abraham and Sarah doubted that their own precious bundle would arrive.

Was God expecting them, as an act of faith and good heart, to do something themselves about their situation? to furnish their human part of the equation? Under the tyranny of such thoughts, Sarah suggested to Abraham, although he was approximately eighty-seven years old and physically "as good as dead" (Hebrews 11:12), that he take her maidservant Hagar in her place in order to try to conceive a child.

Ishmael was born, and for thirteen years God let Abraham and Sarah think that Ishmael was the son of the promise. Ishmael had probably even been told that in time he would inherit everything. One day, however, God sent two messengers to tell Abraham that within one year Sarah would have a child. Sarah laughed at this, and the angel of the Lord heard her and challenged her unbelief.

Sure enough, Isaac, which means "he laughs," was born one year later. Our friend Georgian Banov points out that "whenever you look at a Hebrew person, you are looking at a miracle."

It was clear within a short time that all was not well. Violent sibling rivalry threatened the core of family life as Ishmael taunted Isaac, jealous of the favor Isaac held with Abraham. The two mothers, Hagar and Sarah, grew to resent each other, jealous for their sons' positions in the family. Finally Sarah told Abraham that Hagar and Ishmael had to go because Abraham's firstborn son was a threat to Isaac. God also spoke to the patriarch and instructed him to send them away, but He promised Abraham that He would make a nation out of Ishmael as well. Mercifully God took care of Hagar and Ishmael. He opened a spring for them in the desert and later blessed Ishmael and his descendants because he was Abraham's son.

Abraham's natural descendants today number many millions, but sadly they are divided into two warring camps, the sons of Isaac and the sons of Ishmael, the Arabs, who have been corrupted by a false religion.

Figuratively speaking, Ishmaels are the seemingly wonderful agendas that stand, sometimes for years, in place of God's best. When God waits, there is always a reason. But sometimes it brings out the worst in us. When God waited nearly twenty years to bring His promise to pass, until Sarah and Abraham were good and old, well past childbearing years, God was setting the stage to show his miraculous power. Ishmael was Abraham's attempt to help God when He did not need any help.

Some people are better at Ishmael-creating than others because they are blessed with abilities they can use to glorify God. But anything we do with our abilities is an act of worship, not revival. As God waits to bring His words to pass over our lives, we begin to think that our Ishmaels are the fulfillment of His promises. He may even bless them, as God blessed Abraham's first son, and surround them with supernatural activity, and we nurture these children along—until suddenly the God-initiated comes.

Uh-oh. Within days it is clear that the God-initiated is in direct conflict with the man-generated. The human plan has to go, even though God's blessing seems to have been on it, or it will quench the move of the Holy Spirit.

But by now some people are attached to Ishmael and love him, as the patriarch loved his son. It does not matter to them that Ishmaels not only mock the real but imitate it. They are so used to thinking that Ishmael is the son of the promise that they cannot get used to the paradigm shift.

Pruning is inevitable in the life of any congregation and or person who wants revival to flourish.

In the 1980s a movement began among small churches to pattern themselves after a few nationally known "sophisticated" churches. This meant tailoring Sunday services to appeal to the unenlightened public—people who do not know the Lord. In a nutshell it meant eliminating anything that might offend visitors. Nothing loud or potentially frightening was permitted. Controlled professionalism replaced spontaneity.

Little by little we took away from God His right to offend people if He chose to. It is as though we said, "Holy Spirit, stay in the attic. We don't want You to come out on Sunday mornings. You act like a crazy relative sometimes and You might offend the visitors." The standard of measure became our own comfort zones. Because people rallied to this, even in small churches, we thought it was God's best.

But after all, doesn't the Lord know who the real seekers are? At what point do we plan to bring the "monster" out of the attic, to expose our newcomers to what we really believe? Or do we believe it ourselves anymore? Maybe that is why we need revival!

I believe one reason the Holy Spirit is coming in a way that generates such powerful emotional responses from people is to fly in the face of this movement, and every other tradition, Pentecostal and charismatic included, that tries to control Him. I believe He wants to rescue the Church from its sophisticated grave.

Stuart Bell, leader of a stream of 75 churches in Britain known as Ground Level, tells this story.

One night his son, Andrew, brought a young woman to a renewal service at the church he pastors in Lincoln, England. She had never been to church before. During the ministry time she found herself sandwiched between two people receiving God's presence with loud and embarrassing manifestations. Stuart, who was officiating at the service, worried that the young woman might be offended and never come back.

The service ended. Two weeks passed. Then the young woman returned. Stuart welcomed her to the meeting and talked with her later.

"I wasn't here last week," she said. "I went to a church that was really weird. They were sitting on the benches and everyone was just staring at the front. Then they passed plates around. One guy talked and everyone sang out of books. I wanted to come back to a church with normal people where God is real!"

I believe that progressively more vigorous signs and manifestations will characterize every revival to come. We have not begun to see how God opposes our attempts at controlling Him. And He is going to have fun breaking out of our boxes, even ones we may be unknowingly creating in this move of the Spirit!

Scheduled Christian events are not the same as revival. Nor are seminars, methodology or organizations. Programs of self-effort simply imitate the sovereign work of the Holy Spirit. They are often what we turn to during seasons when the supernatural seems lost.

Heidi and Rolland Baker, missionaries to Mozambique, Africa, have planted more than seventeen hundred churches in that country since being touched by the Holy Spirit in Toronto. Before that experience they had planted three churches in Hong Kong. Then, as the renewal broke out, the Bakers were directed to relocate to Mozambique, where they find themselves co-laboring with Christ in a jet stream of God-initiated activity. "We've done it all without a flow chart," says Heidi, "because the Holy Spirit is doing it."

Although Heidi holds a doctoral degree from King's College in London, she eschews the Western worldly wisdom that has crept into the Church. In their church planting, for instance, the Bakers do not select pastors on the basis of human-generated methods like personality testing. Instead they recognize the anointing and hunger for intimacy with God that sets the leader apart.

Casting Out the Bondwoman

The apostle Paul used the parallel of Isaac and Ishmael when writing to the Galatian church about her backsliding into the Law after receiving Jesus. In reference to the Law, Paul wrote, "Cast out the bondwoman and her son, for the son of the bondwoman shall not be an heir with the son of the free woman" (Galatians 4:30).

As with Abraham and Hagar, the bondwoman that our agendas have become must be cast out or she will do a terrible disservice to the next generation. We will pollute the River and ultimately prevent the Church from enjoying His presence. And without meaning to, we will immunize the next generation against the next supernatural visitation of God.

Driving out the bondwoman from our midst may mean pruning a church of everything you were doing before. Like ripping off a Band-Aid, the quicker, the better. Changing slowly prolongs the pain. Better to do it while people are enjoying the sense of God's presence than to wait until old traditions quench the Spirit and try to do it then. Sometimes people who are unable to make the paradigm shift will leave a church, but it makes room for those who are hungry for what God is doing.

When God first came to us in 1994, we called a moratorium on all our works of service and just soaked in His presence. We were so fearful of quenching the Spirit that we were reticent to initiate anything. Then He called us to rest from our works and enter into His.

God does works that human beings can never do and have not been able to do with all our methods. If we do not drive out the bondwoman, Hagar, from our midst, we will eventually return to works-based methods of "doing church." We will take ourselves out of the current and dry out on the River's bank. But if we nourish revival, Isaac will grow up and become the move of the Spirit, the son of the promise that we have been waiting for, the revival that will eventually touch the ends of the earth.

Know the treasure of the springs of revival. Keep it pure. Now we need to learn not to block its flow.

Let the River Run Free

Ten-year-old Nazarij Dorosh approached me timidly one night at our Friday night renewal meeting. In his hand he held a page he had torn out of *The Weekly Reader*, a newsmagazine for schoolchildren in America. Nazarij said quietly, "I think this is a prophecy."

It was an article entitled "Letting Rivers Run Free" about the Edwards Dam being torn down on Maine's Kennebec River. It explained that dams exist for two reasons: to harness the power of a river and to control the flow. After more than 160 years, scientists have discovered that dams are affecting the proliferation of salmon and trout because they cannot access their breeding grounds in the "cool clear water far up the river." The article explained that power is actually being furnished now by other, more effective sources.

Young Nazarij was right. This *is* a prophecy. Now that revival—our more effective source of power—has come, maybe we need to break down some dams that are harnessing the power, controlling the flow and keeping back the harvest of fish.

BREAKING THE DAM OF COMPARTMENTALIZATION

The number-one mistake a leader can make when God shows up in his church is to separate the renewal from the mainstream of church life. Individuals make this mistake as well. When we compartmentalize the outpouring, we turn it into something we do only at certain times; it is not something we want to see happen all the time.

Compartmentalization is a revival killer! It happens when we do not allow the life-giving flow of God's intimate presence to take center stage in the church program. Instead we confine the outpouring to a service on another night, and we put someone else in charge of it who "has that burden." This implies that participation by the entire church is not necessary. And in so doing we force God into the basement and away from Sunday morning because we do not want what we readily admitted was the Holy Spirit to change our traditions.

Why not? What is so good about the shadow that it cannot give way to the substance?

Churches that say they want revival but are not willing to make it the focus of church life are mystified when it dies out. "If it happens, we'll let it happen," they say, as though it will flourish on its own. They never adopt such a passive approach about other areas of church life, only revival.

Leaders take note: What we send up the flagpole will determine what rallies the troops. Make sure that the crowd you are gathering is drawn by the outpouring of the Spirit, or you will eventually find Ishmael and Isaac, tradition versus life, the old warring against the new. This conflict will dam up the River from flowing. More than at any other time, this revival needs leaders who will allow God's presence to replace lifeless programs born of fruitless striving.

Stop Harnessing the Power

In a move of the Spirit, God wants His power and presence to flow to the ends of the earth in the pure form it came out at the fountainhead. All who come to drink have the same chance to be filled with the pure water from heaven.

The dams we build keep that pure flow from refreshing people who need God's touch. Many in the Body of Christ, because of their own insecurities, want to harness the power of a revival. They will dam up the River, allowing it to flow only when they want, and to flow toward their agendas or programs or the emphases they believe will "get the job done for God." Or they let it seep only through their traditional customs.

In order to remove dams, leaders must answer two hard questions:

> Is your congregation being led by those who place a high value on the renewal?
>
> Do you invite guest speakers who have been thoroughly changed by the outpouring?

If the answers are no, your focus will remain the same and the concentrated power of the revival will dissipate. Letting people who are deeply affected lead is a key to letting people in the church know how important the River is.

Nothing Must Block Its Flow

In the beginning, God gave us two words about guarding the outpouring in our fellowship: *simple* and *flexible*. We were to keep the church calendar uncluttered and be ready to change if we were to keep flowing in the River. If we needed to let go of something, we did. If we needed to be open to inviting speakers we had never had before, we invited them.

One big change for us came in the area of releasing faithful people who were becoming spiritually mature to take responsibility. The Lord spoke to us out of Numbers 11 indicating that He was about to displace some of the authority and anointing onto people in the congregation.

I mentioned two of these earlier. Our children's pastor, Nancy Westerberg, had been a faithful member of the church for twenty years. Her responsibilities increased. Our associate pastor, Bev Watt, who had been a deacon for nearly fifteen years when this all began and who knew our vision, now leads the congregation when we are teaching in other nations. Both Bev and Nancy have hearts to serve and to train and release others into ministry.

We also trained for the prayer team ministry many who had been sitting in our pews. They now move in the powerful anointing the Holy Spirit is pouring out.

Oddly enough, when we were about to initiate cell groups, the Holy Spirit stopped us. He told us, "If you do this now, you will put the fire out." Sure enough, we had chosen people prematurely. Starting cell groups then would have decentralized the fire and separated the burning embers from each other.

God may give different instructions to other pastors; the important thing is to be led by the Holy Spirit. Cell groups may spread the fire in one place and quench it in another place. We cannot imitate what others are doing.

What is the central emphasis in your life and your church's life? Is it the presence of Jesus nurtured by the new outpouring? If not, you are below a dam in the River and the fullness of what God wants for your life will never reach you. The dam must break.

Difficulty arises when leaders who are afraid of the turmoil, the change that revival brings, try to control it. Like someone monitoring a dam's seepage, they decide how much River we will have today. Any time the new mixes with the old, the new always loses out. The Christians who are enjoying revival the most are those who are letting go of control and admitting that they do not know better than God does how to run a church or how much of the flow they need in their lives. They just want more.

Trying to avoid making the decision to "go for it" is just another form of wanting to obtain peace at any price. You will never be happy and will always wonder what might have happened if you had broken the dam and let it flow unhindered.

Why sacrifice a system that works, you may be wondering, for something that may not pan out to be all you wanted? The reason is that there is no reward in heaven for the wood, hay and stubble of self-effort. We will be rewarded for joyful obedience. Knowing that you have risked all for Jesus brings great peace. I have talked to many ministers who are now full of regret that they did not make room for the renewal. Oh, maybe it lasted for a few weeks or a year, but now they are tormented with what might have been had they only kept flowing with it. The cost of trying to go back now may be greater than they or their congregations are willing to pay.

LETTING GOD SET THE AGENDA

Once you resolve to keep the springs of revival flowing, you will begin to see the Holy Spirit produce fruit. People will become so filled with His presence that they will be anxious to give it away regardless of where He leads. We have been shocked at where the River has taken us once we removed everything that stood in the way. One of those places was to prison.

Prior to 1994 I had a rather hardhearted attitude toward people in prison. I believed that criminals belonged behind bars, and I had no intention of visiting them.

Then after *The River Is Here* was published, *Charisma* magazine asked me to write an article. Entitled "Where the River Flows" it spoke of the effects of the Toronto renewal. Inmates in two prisons, one in Alabama and the other in Virginia, read the article and picked up the scent like hound dogs on a trail. Soon we were receiving letters that seemed like Macedonian cries for help.

One letter was especially touching. An inmate had drawn an outline of his hand on a piece of paper and had scrawled a note beneath it: "We know that you could never come to our prison; it's too far away, but we believe that if your prayer team will just lay their hands on this piece of paper the Toronto Blessing will transfer to our prison."

How different, I thought, *from the frowns that greeted me in some upstanding churches when I had mentioned the word* Toronto *from the pulpit.* I knew that we had to go to them.

We obtained approval and a few months later, on Memorial Day weekend in 1997, a team of fourteen people from our church including worship team members and both of our grown children pulled up outside Augusta Correctional Facility in Craigsville, Virginia, a maximum-security facility. I remember feeling fear, not knowing if what we had been given by God would transfer to them. I also had a vague question of whether or not we would survive the weekend.

We left our purses and driver's licenses behind and, in the shadow of razor wire, passed five at a time through the three sets of steel gates that set this maximum-security facility apart from the rest of humanity. And we were not prepared for what we saw.

Three inmates were keeping watch by poking their heads out of the cafeteria door where we would be meeting. They spotted us. "They're here! They're here!" we heard them exclaiming to each other excitedly.

As we entered the room, a crowd of murderers, rapists, child molesters and armed robbers converged on our group. Now, instead of being afraid, we were amazed that they seemed more like elementary school children than hardened criminals.

The three inmates, Greg, Ed and Lee, who were responsible for making sure we had come, rushed up to us. Ed and Greg had already read the copies of *The River Is Here* that we had sent them and had passages of it memorized.

They wanted prayer immediately. "Can we do carpet time?" they pleaded. There was not a fiber of carpet in sight, only the damp tile floor of the prison cafeteria that reeked of pine-scented cleaner. We started praying for them, wondering if the Holy Spirit would touch them. To our amazement, they started receiving, becoming visibly affected as looks of increasing peace and joy swept across their anxious faces.

One inmate, Ernie, fell on the floor and was under the power of God's presence for the remainder of the meeting.

We chose to minister on one of the prevailing themes of this outpouring, the revelation of the Father heart of God. Practically no one there had had a good relationship with his dad.

The inmates were packed into the cafeteria. Some came because it was the first time they had heard live music in years. They loved the songs, the fresh sounds of renewal, songs about intimacy with God and especially "God Is in the House," one of Paul's new ones.

After the message we had only 25 minutes to pray for them since prison services are allowed to last only an hour and a half. One by one, inmates began to fall in response to prayer as the Holy Spirit started filling them. By the time the guards insisted that they return to their cells, some of them were "drunk in the Spirit." Others were hesitant, bracing themselves for further rejection but willing to give it a try.

One of the inmates had used the prison tape recorder to tape the service. By the time we arrived the next evening we learned that a number of inmates had already listened to the tape, circulating it from cell to cell.

On Monday morning we concluded the services and it was time to go. To my amazement our daughter, Sarah, then 21 years old, got up to speak. Then she started to cry. "I feel so sorry for you all," she said. "Some of you never had a chance. God just wants you to feel His love." By this time some of the hard cases standing at the back were in tears. Inmates were saved and a number were beginning to receive the renewal blessing.

As we packed our equipment to leave, I noticed one inmate sitting by himself staring at the guitars. I sat down beside him and he blurted out, "I almost tore this place up on Saturday night. Why does God hate me?"

I found out that his grandmother had just died. He had already lost a child and several other loved ones since he had been put in prison.

I began to tell him about how the Lord had revealed His love to me and that his grandmother did not want to come back because she was in the arms of Jesus. He nodded silently. Then it was time to go.

After we got home, we received an avalanche of letters from the inmates. The Holy Spirit had begun to move in their meetings in the same way He has been moving in our church. People were falling, laughing and soaking in the presence of God. "Charlie is coming to our Bible studies now," one man wrote.

The following week we received a cassette tape from them. The inmates were singing back to us the renewal songs we had taught them. In the middle of "Amazing Grace" we heard a professionally trained voice. A note wrapped around the tape said, "That voice is Charlie's." He had been saved, had begun to receive renewal prayer and had been slain in the Spirit. Before our weekend there, Charlie was a member of the Nation of Islam.

To date we have made ten trips to that prison as well as to prisons in other states. Weekly we receive letters from them. Now we have a whole bevy of intercessors composed of incarcerated angels, former criminals made holy by His presence, who are standing in the gap for what God is doing in the earth.

But suppose we had not determined to keep the springs of revival flowing? Suppose we had not realized the value of this incomparable gift or had not kept it pure? Suppose we had substituted our agenda for the ministry God opened up for us?

We are finding that it is much more fun and fruitful to let God's plans flow than to try to figure out what needs to happen, dam up the River and control its flow.

There is a secret to continuous revival. Here in my husband's words is the way to find it.

Ten

Don't Stop Now!

by Bill Fish

One Sunday morning in March 1989, Melinda gave a prophecy at the end of our meeting. "This will be the year of the opening of the prison to them that are bound behind the Iron Curtain. If you yoke your arm with Mine, you will see a miracle happen. . . ." We did not know that in November of that year the Berlin Wall would be torn down.

The miracle for our church began when we sponsored a thirteen-member Ukrainian Pentecostal family. They were among the first wave of religiously oppressed people that Mikhail Gorbachev released from the then Soviet Union.

For months we planned and worked with government and church agencies to bring the family to this country. Doors opened miraculously. One man donated a house. People from all over Pittsburgh, an area full of second and third generation descendants of Eastern European immigrants, donated furniture and appliances, and our church donated the elbow grease.

In September 1989 Vitali and Maria Dorosh came into our lives with their eleven children, and we fell in love with them instantly. When we asked Vitali why he had risked everything to come, he said, "I want all my children to serve God." We knew then that all our effort had been worth it.

For the next three years we devoted ourselves to them. We took the parents and eleven children to the dentist, enrolled each child in school, found "English as a Second Language" classes and spent hours laughing and talking with them. We thought we were building relationships that would last a lifetime.

By this time other Ukrainian Pentecostal families were moving into the area, but they were more skeptical toward Americans than the Doroshes had been. Typical of the persecuted Church behind the Iron Curtain, they had suffered so long that they braced themselves for continued suffering. I am sure that it was hard for them to believe that our motives were pure. Gradually this attitude affected the Doroshes as well and for a span of about five years we saw them only on rare occasions. This was heartbreaking and one more reason why it seemed that everything we tried to do in those years prior to the outpouring actually produced very little tangible fruit.

Our son, Bill, kept in touch with their son Mike who often came over to visit. We would hear Bill and Mike upstairs arguing over religion. Bill was on the grace page; Mike believed that if he took a cookie from the cookie jar, forgot about it and Jesus Christ returned before he repented of it, then he would go to hell.

Mike was always friendly and had a winsome personality. We could not help accepting him as a "grandson." He sometimes went on family vacations with us. Mike came to our services occasionally, but he had to leave early to make it to the Ukrainian church's service on time.

When revival broke out in our congregation, the Dorosh family was long gone except for Mike. He started coming to the Friday night meeting and allowed the prayer team to pray for him. The Holy Spirit touched him powerfully. Each Friday we would see Mike stretched out on the carpet under the power of the Holy Spirit's presence. For the first time in Mike's life he was feeling God's love and affirmation.

One Friday night Rob Folen, a guest minister who was leading a youth weekend at our church, started to prophesy over various individuals. He picked Mike out of the back row and prophesied: "You are going to be like Moses to your family. You will take a step out of bondage and all your family will be coming with you."

When he spoke those words, Melinda and I looked at each other. We knew what the other was thinking: *He does not know what that is going to take.* We could not imagine anything radical happening to a family so heavily entrenched in tradition and fear.

Within a month, however, we noticed that several of the Dorosh kids were coming to the Friday night meeting and receiving prayer. They would fall under the presence of God and lie there basking in the River of God's glory sometimes for an hour at a time.

Then we noticed other changes taking place in them. They started to smile and wear clothes like regular American teenagers. When worship began, they would be up front dancing with our teens. We were already in awe of the miracle God was doing, but it continued to unfold.

The response of the Ukrainian church to this behavior in the young people was probably predictable; it amounted to persecution. The church forbade Vera, one of Mike's teenaged sisters, to be water baptized. Vera had been saved when the youth attended the Fresh Wind Conference in Toronto where she received a revelation of the grace of God.

When the Ukrainian church refused to baptize Vera, who was so on fire for the Lord, Mike realized that he had had enough. He could not go back. It was too spiritually and emo-tionally stifling. He would begin to feel the Lord's love at the renewal meetings only to go back into an oppressive and fearful atmosphere that condemned him for his behavior.

When Mike made the break, suddenly the air cleared around him. Finally freed from the constant confusion he experienced by being pulled in two such diverse directions, he was now able to discern the Lord's leading.

Mike felt the call to missions. To everyone's surprise, a door opened for him to go back to the Ukraine for two months to help a missionary who had been touched by the Toronto outpouring. Then Mike went to the Toronto School of Ministry and eventually on another mission trip to the Ukraine.

During this time his parents, Vitali and Maria, were won-dering why their children, once so apathetic, were now eager to go to church. And why did they keep talking about what God was doing? They decided to visit the Friday night meet-ing to check it out.

When Vitali walked in the door and saw everyone lying on the floor, he asked God, "Lord, what is 'zis?" The Lord said, "Do you want to know?" Vitali replied, "Yes, I want to know."

Immediately Vitali fell to the carpet, as though someone had pulled his legs out from under him. He could feel the presence of God.

Then Vitali heard people laughing. He said, "Lord, what is 'zis laughing?" The Lord said, "Do you want to know?" Vitali replied, "Yes, I want to know." To everyone's amazement Vitali, who always wept when he prayed, started laughing. And the truth is he has not quit.

Now Vitali comes every Friday to the renewal meeting. Maria has been filled, too, over and over again with God's new wine. They are some of our most inebriated "new wine" drinkers. They cannot seem to get enough. Recently on a Sunday morning Vitali testified, "I'm so glad to have a church where I can just keep drinking the joy of the Lord."

I am glad, too. I am glad that we did not give up a few weeks or months or years after the Blessing came. I am glad it did not seep through our fingers like sand. I shudder to think of the miracles that would not have happened had we given up.

My word to you is this: *Don't stop now!* Here are some tips that we have found to be beneficial to continuing openness to the outpouring of God's presence among us.

If He Has Not Told You to Stop, Keep Going

One Sunday morning in September 1997 I opened the Bible to 2 Kings 13. It tells the story of Elisha, who is sick and about to die. The king of Israel, Jehoash, is paralyzed with fear because the prophet is disappearing from Israel; the Aramaens, his enemies, have not yet been defeated.

Elisha, in what would be one of his last prophetic words, told King Jehoash to open the window. "Now," he said, "take a bow and arrow and release the arrow out the east window, because the Lord is giving you victory today."

This was good news because the Aramaens had already defeated Jehoash once and there were almost no weapons left in his arsenal.

Elisha laid his hands on Jehoash's and they released the arrow together.

"Now," Elisha said, "take the remaining arrows and strike the ground with them."

Elisha told him to strike, but he never told him how many times.

The king struck the ground three times and stopped. Elisha was angry. "You should have struck the ground five or six times and you would have totally defeated Aram and destroyed it; but now you will only defeat them three times."

Here is what I believe God was telling me through that passage. In 1994 when the outpouring of the Holy Spirit started, God put into my hand what some thought was an insignificant arrow. Not everyone thought that the Toronto renewal was connected to revival, but it was. God had put into my hand His arrow of victory. I needed to believe that and to keep striking the ground with both the revelation that God had given me and the new anointing we had received.

In other words, God was telling us through this Scripture to keep going and not stop until He told us to. When I shared this message that September Sunday in 1997, I illustrated it with a handful of aluminum arrows I had bought at Wal-Mart. As I talked about it and illustrated it by striking the ground, the congregation picked up the cadence by stomping the floor with their feet.

People spontaneously came to the pulpit, picked up arrows and began to strike the ground, calling out the names of their loved ones and the prayer burdens God had given them. The service started at ten A.M. and we were there until after two P.M. striking the ground. And you could say that we are still striking. In every service we strike the ground again by keeping the doors open to the thirsty who are coming for refreshing.

I believe that the return of the Dorosh family, for instance, was a gift of God that confirmed our desire to keep going. Our striking the ground was a significant connection between where they were and where God would take them. They needed to begin experiencing this new dimension of the Holy Spirit. We were the place where they could access Him.

As we strike the arrows of the anointing that some call the Toronto Blessing, we are seeing everything God promised us come to pass before our eyes. And as we keep on striking, other doors open, both to prisons in this country and to hungry churches in other nations.

In the beginning I wondered what this Blessing was for. Would it build my church? That is a question every pastor wants answered. God said to us, "I'm going to build My

Church, and I'm going to send out a cadre of happy missionaries." As the people in our congregation keep soaking in His presence, they have boldness and eagerness in believing that God will use them in nations they have never seen. The children in the Lord's quiver are like arrows in the hands of a Mighty Man.

We have other arrows of victory, too, with which we keep on striking. Melinda's books, for instance, are arrows in the hands of the Lord. This one is her sixth. I am amazed that as she keeps soaking in God's presence, He continues to anoint what she did in the past. Letters come from people all over the world who are just now reading what she wrote nine years ago and finding healing and release. It is as though the glory of the Lord is her rearguard, blessing what she did even before renewal started.

We love to view our young people as the Lord's arrows. Before we went to Toronto the first time, our youth group was composed of young kids who came to church either to see their friends or because their parents made them. That has changed now.

The tipping point was when Mike Dorosh inspired other kids in his family to come. Then the Dorosh kids began to witness on the street. They had many "victims"! One was a high school kid named Roy.

Roy Faust had been born in a Hare Krishna commune and delivered by an Amish midwife. His father and mother were divorced. Roy started coming to the Friday night renewal meeting when the Dorosh kids started "advertising" it by word of mouth. The members of the prayer team prayed for him as they prayed for everyone else who needed refreshing: They touched him gently and said, "Come, Holy Spirit." Roy began to feel the presence of God for the first time in his life. The Holy Spirit started touching Roy even before he prayed the prayer of salvation. That is what we call "Presence evangelism."

Now Roy comes to every service. He is in college, a 45-minute drive from the church, but friends in his college town bring him every week. He keeps soaking in the presence of God.

Roy went with us on one of our recent prison trips. With his quiet demeanor, Roy stood in front of the inmates and told how he had missed his earthly father's love his whole life. Then he testified how God had become his Father during this outpouring of the Spirit. When it was time for us to leave, the inmates cheered for Roy. His honest testimony deeply moved them.

So we continue, rejoicing in what God is doing and believing that He will bring all that we have been waiting for.

This is such a vital point. Nothing Melinda has shared in this book will be of any value unless those who read it keep persevering. Perseverance is the key to unlocking most of the treasures of the Kingdom of heaven, including the blessing of revival. A lack of perseverance, on the other hand, is the principal reason why revival has died out in many places. The people or the leaders did not accept the challenge of repetitive obedience. They did not keep going. If there seemed to be a temporary lull, they cast revival aside. How tragic! They have missed most of the fruit God intended them to grow.

Paul said, "Let us not lose heart in doing good, for in due time we will reap if we do not grow weary" (Galatians 6:9). The Holy Spirit has come to give us new courage to keep going until we see everything that He has for us fall from heaven. Maybe our current state is a cloud the size of a man's hand. Or maybe it is the first trip around Jericho's walls, or the first time that blind Bartimaeus cried out, "Jesus, Son of David, have mercy on me!" Perhaps it is Namaan's first dip in the Jordan River.

Do you see how in every one of these cases, the Lord wanted the people involved to do something over and over again? It was an action that seemed to be disconnected from what they needed. But obeying until they saw what God wanted them to see was the key. The only thing that stood between them and victory was being too timid to persevere.

BELIEVE IN WHAT GOD HAS TOLD YOU TO DO

When Elisha told King Jehoash to strike the ground with arrows, it must have seemed foolish. How could this disconnected action determine the outcome of battle? He probably thought, *We're in the middle of a war here. We need chariots and horses. How can one quiver of arrows do any good?*

As with so many other examples in Scripture, we see here the human heart laid bare. Yet this action was meant to be a prophetic symbol of what God intended to do. I believe that Jehoash struck the ground three times simply to pacify the prophet. He did not understand the significance of the request and so he was halfhearted about it. Unless you believe that you hold God's arrow of victory, you will be halfhearted or timid and you will give up too soon.

When God told me to move from Texas to Pittsburgh in 1976, I did not understand why He would call me to a city I had never seen, the birthplace of the charismatic renewal. There were already great men and women of God here; I could not see how our coming here was of value to the Kingdom's advancement. Melinda was not all that sure, either. She did not want to leave her southern roots, but because she loves me and believes in me, she came willingly.

Six weeks after we arrived in Pittsburgh, the denomination we were a part of withdrew our funding because of our charismatic experience. Everything about it seemed wrong, but because there was nothing else to do, we just kept going.

When you do not know what else to do, I believe that God wants you to do what you already know to do. I did not know that He was teaching me to persevere no matter what.

Eighteen years went by. When I first heard that laughter had broken out in Toronto, I did not understand what it had to do with the moving of the Holy Spirit. I was like Namaan, the leprous Syrian, so in need of God's River but not understanding why I needed to dip seven times in what God was pouring out in Toronto. Namaan almost did not go to the River at Elisha's command. He became angry and said, "I thought, 'He will surely come out to me and . . . wave his hand over the [diseased] place and cure the leper'" (2 Kings 5:11).

How often sentences that begin with "I thought" get us into trouble! Getting into the Jordan River and dipping seven times cured Namaan's leprosy. He finally believed the prophet's word and did what God told him to do as many times as it took, even though it looked stupid.

Does looking stupid pose a problem for you? If so, you are not alone.

Take Your Cue from God, Not Others

One day when we kids were swimming at the beach, my cousin suddenly found himself being dragged out to sea by the current. Although many adults were swimming nearby, he did not cry out for help. From the beach my father saw that he was in trouble and swam out quickly to rescue him.

Why didn't he yell for help? He later confessed that he was more worried about what we would think of him than he was of drowning. That is the power of peer pressure.

I could not have kept going with the renewal if I had looked too long and hard at what others, even other faithful Christians, were doing. One of our friends from another country recently remarked how the current move of the Spirit had swept through his country seven years before because of unity that was left from the charismatic renewal. Within a year, however, one by one, each leader started to pull back. They did not want to keep going if it meant being different from the others.

It is easy to be distracted by peer pressure. If others get bored with renewal, we follow suit. Or if they are not persuaded that what we are doing is from God, we will wind up explaining ourselves to people who really only want us to conform to their ideas.

Sometimes pastors learn that it is their own church members who are not able to comprehend what the Holy Spirit is doing. I am willing to talk to anyone who is willing to listen and discuss what is going on with this renewal, but in the end I am committed to going where God is leading us. I do not want anyone to be offended needlessly, but I have to remember that Jesus offended some people by what He said and did. I need to keep striking the ground in obedience even if no one else understands right now.

In order to persevere you must determine not to take your cue from others. Wield what God has put in your hand even if it seems insignificant. Decide that you really want God's River. You must be certain because its current will carry you and you may feel out of control as you surrender to the flow. It may take you places where you do not want to go.

What God is doing in local churches through this move of the Holy Spirit is radical—and He is causing adults and young people to become radical about their faith. What does it look like to walk into church and see everyone lying on the floor? It looks strange, just as Elisha's arrows of victory did. This is not about what our peers think but what God thinks.

STRENGTHEN YOURSELF BY SOAKING IN THE RIVER

Melinda has made this point, but I want to mention it again because it is so very important: In order to keep going, you have to have a strength that does not come from anywhere but soaking in the presence of God. As I shared earlier, I had to learn how to open my heart to the Holy Spirit during this outpouring. I did not know how in the beginning, but God taught me.

One of the most important ways that a church can persevere is for the pastor and leaders to keep receiving the waves of God's presence that come in each service. If I fail to do this, I will dry out standing in the River watching everyone else get touched.

This is about loving God with your whole heart and your neighbor as yourself and, for me as pastor, teaching other people to have their own intimate relationships with God. Whenever I feel dry myself, it is hard to tell others about intimacy with God. My faithfulness to keep soaking lets the congregation know that even the pastor needs what God is pouring out; no one is exempt.

Soaking in God's presence gives me the strength to keep striking the ground and not grow weary. It is the joy of the Lord that Nehemiah talked about. Feasting on the presence of God is like manna from heaven. If we keep eating, it is enough to get us across the Jordan.

EMPLOY THE POWER OF PROPHETIC INTERCESSION

Early in the renewal, some of the women in our church journeyed to Toronto and attended an intercessory prayer meeting there. For the first time, they learned to pray by asking God to show them pictures and Scriptures of what He wanted them to pray about. The next week our prophetic intercessory ministry was born. Before this I had always been skeptical of intercessors; I had seen this ministry used to usurp authority. But this was different.

Since that first meeting, as many as one-third of the people in our church, men and women, come regularly on Monday nights to pray. Our associate pastor, Bev Watt, facilitates the prayer meetings. Before the outpouring began I could not have paid people to come to meetings at night, much less prayer meetings, and when they did, the prayers would have had little fervency.

As people attend the comfortable, informal meetings and share the pictures and thoughts that God gives them, they are learning to hear from God more clearly. They are always encouraged to discover that the Holy Spirit is weaving similar threads in the minds and hearts of others who are present.

One night as Melinda and I taught a class on prophecy in our school of ministry, Sheryl Fedore was surprised to see in her mind's eye a picture of Melinda and me on a Viking ship. Not one to seek the limelight, she quietly raised her hand and shared what she had seen. We were all shocked the next morning when Melinda and I opened our e-mail and found an invitation for us to spread the fire in Norway.

In teaching us about prophetic prayer, the Lord has also been showing us the power of prophetic actions. These are symbolic gestures that help us express ourselves to God, just like the arrows of victory that King Jehoash used to strike on the ground. We use a wonderful variety of prophetic actions. They are like offerings to God of our willingness to do the unusual if that is what it takes to see friends and loved ones saved.

Sometimes, for instance, we visit sites in the city and pray. On a cold night recently, some of our more eager members went to the point in Pittsburgh where the Monongahela and Allegheny Rivers form the headwaters of the Ohio. They prayed and then actually threw tea into the river. By this action, which was reminiscent of a revolution in this country centuries ago, they symbolized the fact that the Lord is starting a spiritual revolution in Pittsburgh.

Another time a few of our members drove through the Jewish sector of the city. Each time they passed a synagogue, someone stood up through the sunroof of the car and blew a shofar as a prayer to God to bring in their true Year of Jubilee and bring them to salvation.

It is not unusual to me anymore to come into the sanctuary and find what I call "intercessory artifacts" on the platform and the walls. They are like arrows of victory. We have a shovel hanging on one wall that represents our willingness to dig a well of revival. Tied to it are shipping tags with prayer requests from every member of our congregation. We know that a day is coming when God is going to leave no stone unturned and our loved ones are going to be saved. God will be "shipping" us the answers.

My wife, a Texan, bought a picture at the Alamo of Col. William B. Travis drawing a line in the sand the night in 1836 before all his men perished defending it. The caption reads, "Freedom fighters from around the world." We hung it on the church wall after Ian Ross, one of the Toronto itinerants, gave us a word about commitment.

Melinda is always saying about this move of the Spirit, "It's time to push your poker chips to the middle of the table." So recently I bought a piece of wood, stained it and glued poker chips at the center to remind us that what God is doing is worth everything we have. It is sitting on the platform, too.

We collect bottled water from other nations, symbolic of the revival wells we want God to spring up there. We gather spadefuls of dirt from places that need prayer. On a large sheet we write the names of people we want to see saved.

We amassed a large selection of percussive instruments such as drums and staffs. During the worship, young and old strike the floor with the staffs as a symbolic gesture that we want God to send more of Himself and we will not stop striking the ground until He comes.

Each Sunday morning young people and adults gather downstairs to intercede before the service. Our children's pastor, Nancy Westerberg, leads that meeting. They play drums and ask God to give them prophetic pictures about what He wants them to pray for.

While these pieces of "non-biblical" church furniture remind us to keep striking the ground, this may not be something that every congregation is supposed to do. God will give you your own arrows as you pray. This outpouring has affected our corporate prayer life like nothing I ever heard about in seminary!

We are not alone in this. Wherever we go we find churches that the Holy Spirit is leading in a similar manner. We have met people in other countries and people in distant states who have all had the same prompting from the Holy Spirit to intercede in this manner. It has little to do with the outward accouterments and a lot to do with the hunger people now have to pray.

Note, however, that we do not ever want to regress into the symbolic. We want the substance who is Jesus, not the shadow. We want revival, not symbols of it. But over and over again, prophetic ministers who come to our services confirm what we are doing and see it as having prophetic significance. We will understand more when God reveals the next pieces of our lives. Prophetic intercession and prophetic action encourage our church not to stop.

MAINTAIN THE FOCUS ON RENEWAL

A small, seemingly insignificant place called Azusa Street in Los Angeles, California, became the birthplace of the Pentecostal outpouring in 1906. In its day it was ridiculed or overlooked by those who missed that powerful work of God. Those who were affected by it endured persecution, and their lives were changed forever.

The Azusa Street revival sparked a worldwide move of the Spirit, which continues today. Millions of Pentecostal and charismatic Christians can trace their roots to Azusa Street. During the outpouring thirteen thousand people from all over Los Angeles and the world came to its doors.

I wonder what would have happened had the people maintained their focus and stayed in awe of what God was doing instead of falling into factions and watching the revival dissipate. Would the earth be won by now?

It is vital to keep the attention focused on what God is doing.

I have never been the kind of pastor who comes up with a new idea to try every week. My flaw is the other extreme: I just continue to do what I did before. But God is using my weakness for His purposes. It is a move of God custom-made for me! God has called me to stand in the gap, and standing is something I can do. It is my way of striking the ground. I simply continue to do what God has told me to do, trusting that He is positioning our congregation and me for whatever He wants to do in the future.

Jesus said in Matthew 7:7–8, "Ask, and it will be given to you; seek, and you will find; knock, and it will be opened to you. For everyone who asks receives, and he who seeks finds, and to him who knocks it will be opened." In the Greek all those words indicate that the action begins at one point in time and continues. Paul uses the same kind of verb when he tells us to be filled with the Holy Spirit. We are to keep asking, seeking and knocking and being filled.

Jesus never said anything about stopping. There is never a maximum amount of faith, but there is a minimum. How often in the past I missed what God wanted for me because I did not persist until I saw the fullness of all He had promised!

Our British friend Stuart Bell emphasized these words to our congregation one evening: "Don't stop now!" he exclaimed. Our worship leader has written a song by that title. Not only are we singing about it, we have made the decision that we are not going to stop. It is just too wonderful.

I shudder to think of the fruit we would not have seen had we stopped soon after the outpouring began. Over half the members of our church would not be here, their lives would never have been affected and the fruit God wanted to produce would never have come. The Doroshes would not be here and Roy might not be saved. Nor would people like Donna Bernd, whose grieving heart is being healed. Being a pastor, it saddens me to think of the sheep that would have never found their way to the fountain. Or the people in India and Africa and the prisons in this country who would never have experienced the wonderful presence of God.

There is a gap between what we are now experiencing and what is to come. If we stop striking the ground with the arrow of victory God gave us, we will lose our focus and be distracted into other things, and I believe we can lose the Blessing. I have seen it happen in other churches, and I do not want it happening to mine.

I believe that if I teach this flock to persevere in the divine expectancy that has come through this outpouring of the Holy Spirit, we will indeed "inherit the Land."

Eleven

Getting Ready for More

It was well past four A.M. I fashioned a pillow out of my wadded-up coat and the faded blanket the conductor had given me. I propped myself up on one elbow trying to see beyond the glass window of the train bound from Nagaland to Guwahati, India, where we would catch the plane home. It was too dark to see anything.

Bill was sleeping in the berth above, but I could not sleep. After four days of meetings we were leaving tired but full. The River had broken on the Naga tribes and the trip had been well worth the efforts of our team.

Now a young pastor named Simon of the Dimasa tribe was accompanying Bill and me on the eight-hour train trip back to Guwahati. Simon saw me awake and urged me to go back to sleep. I told him it was useless, so he slid into the seat next to me. What he said next, I will always remember.

"There's a village in my province," he said. "They will not let their fires die out because a king has lit them." The fires he spoke of have been burning without interruption for years. They are tended by villagers who treasure what they think is a sacred flame.

Simon did not know that he was speaking prophetic words of confirmation. Six years earlier God had spoken to us to "keep the fire lit, for it will catch on round about." I knew what God was telling me through Simon. He wanted me to keep the fire lit that He had kindled in my heart. He did not want me to let it die. Not in me, not in our church nor in anyone who would listen.

Revival is a fire that can only be lit by God Himself. We cannot light the sacred flame regardless of how hard we try. Instead, like the priests in the Temple of Solomon who watched the fire fall, we can only treasure it and tend it. I hope that by now you are beginning to understand how. And I pray that the Lord is speaking directly to you in your situation, telling you how to treasure His presence in your life and in your church.

This book has been about stewardship of the greatest thing in the earth today, the presence of God. I do not know about you, but I want to receive more. His presence is so wonderful that I can only imagine that this is a delightful foretaste of another Kingdom breakthrough that is about to happen.

We have been laughing until we cannot stop, weeping from gratitude and soaking as long as we can take in the God who has no limit on how much of Himself He will pour out. All of this is having the effect of softening the heart of anyone who positions himself in the River. With every laugh and tear there has come a precious deposit, a tangible sense of the Father's love. How could there be anything worth more than this?

I also believe that just as Boaz had his servants drop grain on purpose for Ruth to glean, so this current outpouring is dropped on purpose for anyone who will pick it up. He has made Himself accessible to us, feeding us so that our spiritually famished souls will follow where He is leading—not only to more but to an abundance of more. I believe that is why one of the watchword prayers of what God has already been doing is, "More, Lord!"

Entering into the "more" we have all been longing for will come if we wait for it expectantly. I believe that this phase of the outpouring has been a test to see how we would recognize and treasure what He sends out of heaven, even if we do not understand it or if we find it inconvenient or even costly. He wants to know that we love Him enough to do anything for Him.

So how do we prepare for what is ahead?

POSITION YOURSELF FOR BLESSING

Two years after the outpouring began, Peter Lyne, a leader from Great Britain who now lives in New Zealand, visited our church. Peter began to prophesy this word: "Position yourselves for blessing." As I mentioned at the opening of this book, we received prophecy after prophecy about Rivers and Blessings before the move of the Spirit broke out in Toronto.

Looking back now, I believe that I probably just needed to live long enough to see these prophecies come to pass. Now, however, I am seeing them fulfilled, and I am paying closer attention to what the Holy Spirit is saying about the future because I realize that He is preparing me for what lies ahead. And because of what He is doing now, I have more faith that there is more.

Paying attention to the prophetic word means that you will have great joy when you see that God is faithful to what He says. I remember the late John Garlington prophesying in May 1982 about this move of God. He laughed and spoke in tongues and began to cry out, "I will fill your mouths with laughter and you will laugh in the face of the enemy!" It is really true that God does not do anything without revealing it to His servants the prophets. If we do not despise prophesying, we will be in a better position for blessing.

If you keep soaking in what God is pouring out, I believe your heart will stay soft. You will find yourself receiving any blessings that God will pour out in the future because your soft heart will make you humble enough to receive.

Oh, how I wish now that my heart had not been so hard and skeptical in early 1994! I missed almost an entire year of this wonderful Blessing because my heart was too proud. I have learned through this never to say "God always does this" or "God never does that." Those kinds of statements hardened my heart and made me arrogant enough to keep me out of the revival.

Stay Hungry for More of Him

If I had to pick one event that brought me into the Blessing, it would be the hunger of a woman who testified in Toronto. Her head was shaking violently. Everything in me wanted to grab her head and tell her to stop shaking it.

But although her outward manifestation of God's presence annoyed me, what she said called out to me. "A year ago, my husband and I were chronic TV watchers. We didn't even want to go to church. But in January, one Sunday night, someone called and said, 'Get down to the church. God's moving.'

"So we went down to the church," she said, "and we've been back every night since then. And tonight I'm more in love with Jesus than I ever have been in all of my life."

I thought, *Oh, God! I don't care if I have to shake my head, roll on the floor or cry until there are no more tears. I don't care if nothing happens to me. All I want is my first love passion for Jesus, and I'll do anything to get it back.* Today my testimony is this: "I'm more in love with Jesus than I ever have been in all of my life." The Holy Spirit used that woman's testimony to make me hungry for more of Jesus' love. In my opinion, He may have sent this whole thing just for me.

I believe that God is making people hungry for more because He is going to send more. He wants us to be continually hungry and thirsty for more of Him. He wants us to press on to know Him ever more intimately.

So What Will "More" Look Like?

I believe "more" will be exactly that. God will begin to pour out on the multitudes what He is pouring out on a few. The disciples knew the intimate presence of the Holy Spirit as Jesus breathed on them in the Upper Room, but at Pentecost the Lord refilled them and multiplied the experience—first on 120 and by the end of the day on 3,000. Now multiplied millions of people worldwide have received the baptism in the Holy Spirit.

Revival begins like the leaven of the Kingdom of heaven. It seems tiny, almost microscopic in comparison with the effect it is about to have. What happened in Toronto, or at Pentecost for that matter, is still having an effect years after the initial outbreak.

In any new outpouring of the Holy Spirit, God places more leaven on earth and accelerates the pace at which the news of Jesus and His Kingdom spreads. Fresh moves of the Spirit are coming at a more rapid rate. In the twentieth century, we saw the Welsh revival, Azusa Street and the Pentecostal revival, the Latter Rain and healing revivals, the charismatic renewal, the Third Wave, the outpouring in Argentina and now the River breaking out in Toronto and beyond. The impact of revival is multiplying all over the world, flowing like a great River from the Father's throne.

What Is about to Happen?

As the Church receives the revelation of the heavenly Father's love and the Bridegroom's passion for her, she will awaken from slumber and light the way for the lost to come to the wellsprings of life.

We are on the brink of a worldwide awakening; it has already begun. Future church historians will point to key places in the Western hemisphere such as Toronto, Argentina and Pensacola where this outpouring began. But what has happened there will be eclipsed by what the Lord is about to do. These sites of outpouring have sown seeds in the earth. The enemy has tried to cover them over saying, "That's not God," but what has been sown is beginning to sprout.

This planting will have an exponential effect. It will begin to escalate rapidly all over the world. Churches large and small will be revolutionized by hunger for more of Jesus' love. They will not care how long the services last or even who is preaching. The Holy Spirit will inundate both the two or three and the thousands gathered in His name. Unity we have never imagined will grow under a hovering canopy of God's presence.

I believe that the spiritual hunger for more of Jesus will turn into conviction, and people all over the world will make their way to places where they can find bread. If you maintain your God-initiated hunger for Jesus, then your friends and relatives will approach you and ask you what is going on with you, because God is going to send the same hunger on them. They will want Jesus and not know why. People everywhere, from the humblest home to high places in government, will experience this and long for Jesus' love.

Unbelievers who are invaded by this divinely inspired spiritual hunger will not be offended. In fact, the outward manifestations will become more pronounced as the days progress toward Jesus' coming. We will see an increase in the frequency and magnitude of signs and wonders that will make people fall on their faces and worship Jesus. People will want Him desperately. And then He will feed them and they will taste and see that the Lord is good.

In places where it seems that the River has receded, a flash flood will come and wash away manmade structures and everything else that stands in God's way. Jezebel will fall from her window and be devoured as God's authority takes its rightful place. We will begin to see the flood, rain and the wind of the Holy Spirit assault houses of worship all over the world, and those not built on the Rock will experience upheaval. In fact, some structures will be broken down so that the God-pitched tabernacles can be true houses of His glory, and we will not care because the precious glory of His presence will be the only thing that matters. What has been called a River will become a Flood. The only way to prepare is to make yourself low before the coming wave.

God can do anything, and we need to be ready for it. We need to ask to see the way He sees so that we can recognize the next wave.

GIVE AWAY WHAT GOD HAS ALREADY GIVEN YOU

It is as though we are serving a master who has gone away on a journey and promised to return. To some in the Church He has given five gold coins, to others He has given two and to others only one. When He comes back I wonder if He will ask us, "What did you do with what I sent in '94?"

Jesus said, "To everyone who has, more shall be given, and he will have an abundance; but from the one who does not have, even what he does have shall be taken away" (Matthew 25:29). The principle of stewardship is taking what God gives you, investing it and seeing His Kingdom multiply.

When Bill and I were in the Ukraine, I heard God say to me, "You and Bill are like migrant farm workers, laboring wherever the harvest is coming in." I believe if we follow the River to the ends of the earth, we will find the harvest ready for reaping. Never mind grieving over why it is not appearing where you are; go find where it is appearing and set your hand to it. I do not believe we will finish reaping until all these things are fulfilled.

This dimension of His presence that we call "revival" is like a slippery bar of soap. If you try to grasp it, it will squirt out of your hand, but if you hold it in an open palm you can keep it and others can touch it, too. Giving away the Blessing is believing that what God has given you is worth giving away. In the parable of the talents, the slave with one talent spent more of his time worrying about why he had not been given more than he did about doing something with what he had. He despised what he had been given.

Are you still soaking in the love and the grace of God, or did you stop? Are you still in awe of all the wonder of this move of God, or did you walk away from it? Are you giving away the Blessing, or did you bury it in the ground and say, "Oh, well, it was only a renewal. I want revival!"? If so, you need to get back into the River and reposition yourself for more.

The Endless Revival

I believe that we were prophesying when we named this move of the Spirit "the River" because rivers never end. How can there be an end to the River of His love and grace? There will not be unless we dam it up or get out of it ourselves.

I have mentioned that early in the revival I heard people saying over and over, "Come, Holy Spirit!" It is the prayer that has invited the Holy Spirit to touch millions in this outpouring. Soon another prayer began to well up in me: "Keep coming, Holy Spirit!"

I often wonder if this is the time when the Spirit and the Bride will cry out in their longing for Jesus to "Come!" If it is, at some point there will be no more that He can give us without bodily coming Himself.

Bibliography

DeArtega, William. *Quenching the Spirit.* Lake Mary, Fla.: Creation House, 1992.

Dubay, Thomas. *Fire Within.* San Francisco: Ignatius Press, 1989.

Edwards, Jonathan. *Jonathan Edwards on Revival.* Carlisle, Penn.: Banner of Truth Trust, 1994.

Finney, Charles G. *Finney on Revival.* Edited by E. E. Shelhammer. Minneapolis: Bethany House Publishers, 1994.

Fowler, Gene. "There's Something in the Water: Old Texas Spas." *Texas Highways Magazine* 45, no. 2 (February 1998): 4–13.

Gladwell, Malcolm. *The Tipping Point: How Little Things Can Make a Big Difference.* London: Little, Brown and Company, 2000.

Hyatt, Eddie. "Let Go and Let the River Flow." *Spread the Fire* magazine 4, no. 6 (December 1998): 13–15.

Hyatt, Eddie. *2000 Years of Charismatic Christianity: A 21st Century Look at Church History from a Pentecostal/Charis-*

matic Perspective. Dallas: Hyatt International Ministries, 1998.

Liardon, Roberts. *God's Generals.* Laguna Hills, Calif.: Albury Publishing, 1996.

Mears, Kenneth, Simon Thurley, and Clare Murphy. *The Crown Jewels.* London: The Historical Royal Palaces Agency, 1994.

McIntyre, Valerie. *Sheep in Wolves' Clothing: How Unseen Need Destroys Friendship and Community and What to Do About It.* Grand Rapids, Mich.: Baker Book House, 1999.

Morphew, Derek. *Breakthrough: Discovering the Kingdom.* Cape Town, South Africa: Vineyard International Press, 1998.

Mullen, Grant W. *Why Do I Feel So Down When My Faith Should Lift Me Up?* Tonbridge, England: Sovereign World Ltd., 1999.

Wallis, Arthur. *In the Day of Thy Power.* Fort Washington, Penn.: Christian Literature Crusade, 1956, 1990.

Melinda Fish and her husband, Bill, are senior pastors of Church of the Risen Saviour in Trafford, Pennsylvania (near Pittsburgh). Melinda is editor of *Spread the Fire* magazine, published bimonthly by Toronto Airport Christian Fellowship, Toronto, Canada, site of the revival known as the Father's Blessing. Melinda is the author of six books published by Chosen Books. Bill and Melinda are the parents of two grown children who are also serving the Lord in full-time ministry.